Afloat in America

Afloat In America

Two enthusiasts explore the United States and Canada by waterway and rail

by
Charles and Alice Mary Hadfield

DAVID & CHARLES
Newton Abbot London North Pomfret (Vt)

Hadfield, Charles
Afloat in America.
1. North America – Description and travel – 1951 –
I. Title II. Hadfield, Alice Mary
917'.04'53 E41
ISBN 0–7153–7910–0

Library of Congress Catalog Card Number 79-52486

Set in 11 on 13 point Baskerville
by Northern Phototypesetting Company, Bolton
and printed in Great Britain
by A. Wheaton & Company Limited, Exeter
for David & Charles (Publishers) Limited
Brunel House Newton Abbot Devon

Published in the United States of America
by David & Charles Inc.
North Pomfret Vermont 05053 USA

Contents

Preface

This is the story of a special-interest holiday. For years we had explored the inland waterways of Britain, as also many in Europe, but we had never seen the canals and great navigable rivers of north America, and conviction grew that we had better go before we got any older. So we went, and because we are almost as fond of railways as of waterways, we decided to move by train whenever we could not travel by boat.

In the three months we gave ourselves, we travelled some 8,000 miles within the eastern United States and Canada: 5,000 on inland waterways, 1,800 on rails and 1,200 by car. We also flew three times on internal air services.

There are many Americas and Canadas. We have written about one of them, as accurately as we could. 'We speak as we find.' It is only one, but in itself it is real and good. We therefore hope that readers will find interest and amusement in our adventures and, if elderly, perhaps be encouraged by them not to feel too old to plan special-interest holidays of their own. They will find their own Americas and Canadas, as we did, and the same warm friendliness and welcome.

We have used some of Robert Legget's pictures in Chapter 6. Our grateful thanks go to him.

ALICE MARY HADFIELD CHARLES HADFIELD

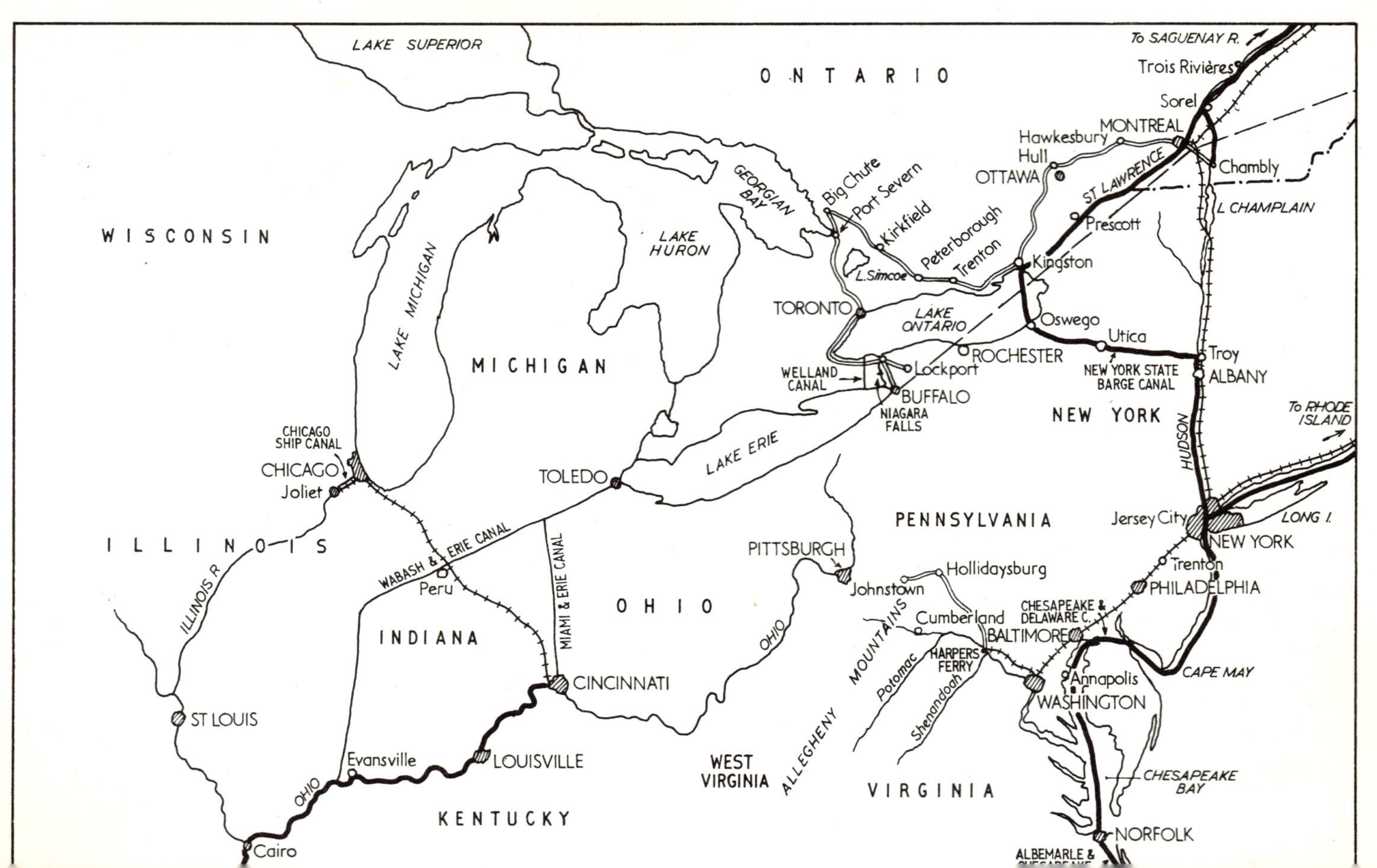
LAKE SUPERIOR
ONTARIO
To SAGUENAY R.
Trois Rivières
Sorel
MONTREAL
Hawkesbury
Hull
OTTAWA
Chambly
ST LAWRENCE
L CHAMPLAIN
Prescott
GEORGIAN BAY
Big Chute
Port Severn
Kirkfield
Peterborough
Trenton
Kingston
L.Simcoe
WISCONSIN
LAKE HURON
LAKE MICHIGAN
MICHIGAN
TORONTO
LAKE ONTARIO
Oswego
Utica
Troy
ALBANY
ROCHESTER
Lockport
NEW YORK STATE BARGE CANAL
WELLAND CANAL
BUFFALO
NIAGARA FALLS
NEW YORK
To RHODE ISLAND
HUDSON
CHICAGO SHIP CANAL
CHICAGO
Joliet
TOLEDO
LAKE ERIE
LONG I.
Jersey City
NEW YORK
PENNSYLVANIA
ILLINOIS
WABASH & ERIE CANAL
Peru
MIAMI & ERIE CANAL
PITTSBURGH
Hollidaysburg
Johnstown
Trenton
PHILADELPHIA
ILLINOIS R
OHIO
MOUNTAINS
Cumberland
CHESAPEAKE & DELAWARE C.
BALTIMORE
INDIANA
HARPERS FERRY
Potomac
Annapolis
CAPE MAY
CINCINNATI
Shenandoah
WASHINGTON
ST LOUIS
ALLEGHENY
Evansville
LOUISVILLE
WEST VIRGINIA
CHESAPEAKE BAY
VIRGINIA
OHIO
KENTUCKY
NORFOLK
ALBEMARLE &
Cairo

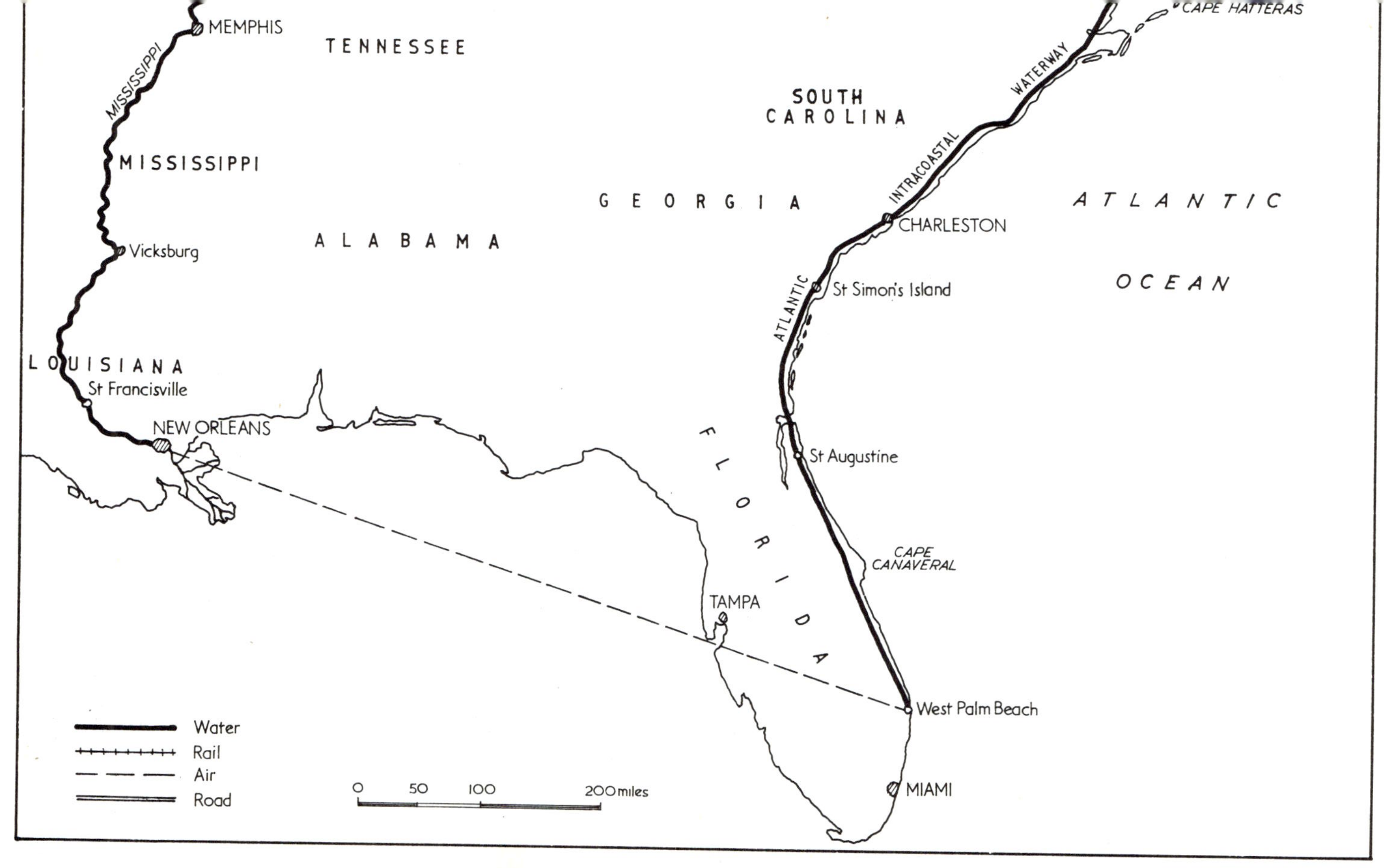
MEMPHIS
TENNESSEE
MISSISSIPPI
MISSISSIPPI
Vicksburg
ALABAMA
LOUISIANA
St Francisville
NEW ORLEANS
GEORGIA
SOUTH CAROLINA
INTRACOASTAL
WATERWAY
ATLANTIC
CAPE HATTERAS
CHARLESTON
St Simon's Island
St Augustine
FLORIDA
CAPE CANAVERAL
TAMPA
West Palm Beach
MIAMI
ATLANTIC
OCEAN
Water
Rail
Air
Road
0
50
100
200 miles

This book is dedicated to our first friends in America, the staff of the coffee-house at the Midland Hotel, Chicago, especially Lucille, Toni and 'Mr Johnson'

Chapter 1

Railway Prelude: Chicago to Cincinnati

'You'll love America', said Harold, 'once you're past immigration. They are surly brutes.'

'Chicago', said the Iranian in the departure lounge at Heathrow, 'they're unfriendly there. You want to be alert in the streets.'

Diffidently we presented our passports and immigration forms at O'Hare airport.

'How long are you staying?'

'Three months, in the States and Canada', we chorused.

'Why?'

'We're authors, and we plan to write a book about your waterways.'

'Is that so? You write? Well, have a good time.'

'Are you carrying any tools of a trade?' the girl asked at Customs – a trick question to anyone proposing to earn money illegally.

'We're authors.' She smiled. 'No pens, no paper?'

'Heavy suitcases? Don't you worry, sir – I'll look after you', said the negro porter. 'Have a good holiday', he told us, as we opened the Yellow Cab door.

'Why Chicago?' asked the Italian-sprung taxi-driver.

'Because of the Chicago Ship Canal', Charles answered. 'It leads to the Mississippi, and I want to see it where it starts, in Lake Michigan.'

'Is that so? And you've come from England to see it?'

'Yes.'

'Well – have a good time.'

'You come from England', said the fresh, eager lad who collected the dirty plates behind the coffee-house counter; 'whereabouts?'

'London.'

'Oh, I'd like to see the Queen – but it's so big, I'd never find my way around.'

'Ask for Trafalgar Square', we said, 'she lives just down the street.'

Next morning we came down to the American Breakfast. Good breakfasters ourselves, we gazed happily at the coffee-house menu, which offered all the usual things, but also such mouth-waterers as 'Golden Waffles with Bacon or Sausage, served with Warm Syrup and Butter' or 'Two Country Fresh Eggs (Any Style), Tasty Top Sirloin Steak, Hashed Brown Potatoes with Buttered Toast', as well as five kinds of fluffy omelette.

No diffident visitor to the States can survive breakfast without liking the country. Perky waitresses are fast and cheerful: 'Hullo, folks, what can I get you?' Coffee appears as soon as one sits down, and keeps on appearing until one leaves. And you may find 'Outstanding American Women' on the sugar packets, among whom we especially took to Carry Nation. 'She fought for Prohibition with a hatchet, a sack full of rocks or an iron bar. She was hated and feared as she swept through the saloons of Kansas smashing bottles and destroying bars.' Outstanding indeed. 'Where wert thou, brother?' we felt like asking any males of Kansas who survived her onslaught. And if one pauses to look around, the sight of a substantial citizen putting away three pancakes and a couple of fried eggs, all outlined in bacon and covered in nose-twitching syrup, sends one contentedly back to one's plate.

We came to miss English bacon (American is to our taste too thin, always streaky, and over-cooked) and English marmalade, but we loved the speed, the colour and smell, the lashings of coffee, and the cheerful phrase that accompanies service: 'You're welcome', and payment of the bill: 'Have a good day!'.

From the 103rd floor of the Sears Building, 1,450ft high and the tallest in the world, the lake shore spread away north and east. Inland we could see the line of the Chicago River, soon dividing into the North and South branches, the latter running past the building. By the river's mouth Fort Dearborn had been built in 1803 as a defence against the Indians. But Chicago began to grow when in 1827 Congress donated alternate sections of land on either side of a proposed 95-mile-long Illinois & Michigan Canal that would join this Chicago River to the Des Plaines River to the south, this in turn leading by way of the Illinois River to the Mississippi. Thus the Great Lakes would be linked to the Gulf of Mexico. Sales of this land, to raise money for construction, began in 1830 when Chicago had one hundred inhabitants; the canal was started six years later and opened in 1848.

Far below us on the North branch, just past the junction, a road-bridge was rising for a tug pushing a barge.

'What are you looking at?' asked our neighbour. We showed him. It started an interest in his group. All together we pursued the barge round three sides of the viewing deck, anxiously forecasting whether the bridges that it came to, each with its own control-cabin, would have to be raised, or whether the load could squeeze beneath. Indeed, that barge-tow symbolised Chicago's origin, as did the Sears Tower its present.

We rode the 'L' the day we had trouble with American plumbing. A single revolving handle controlled the shower, hot or cold, off or on. First we had been pinned to the bathroom wall by the force of the jet; then had filled the bath within an inch of the top with boiling water, while we wildly thought of ringing up the Fire Department, the police and the British consul, before we found which way to turn the handle to 'off'. So we needed to relax.

We knew that the Loop was an oval of railway tracks enclosing the city centre, but nothing else had prepared us for the Chicago Elevated. The San Francisco cable-cars are a tourist attraction – why not the Chicago 'L'? What glorious tracery of sun-patterned old iron stands above Wabash Avenue and Lake Street, Wells and Van Buren, the original Loop completed in 1897! What delicate iron stairways to stations decorated with iron tracery, each painted a different colour, with iron footbridges rising still higher to cross the elevated tracks!

The Chicago Elevated: 'glorious tracery of sun-patterned old iron . . .'

We climbed happily to Adams/Wabash and took a ticket to the Elevated's western extension at 95th Street. First we trundled noisily over the older tracks, then in our crowded car ran fast past Chinatown and the baseball stadium of the Chicago White Sox, where at its own station (35/Sox) many of the passengers got out to see the coming game. At 95th we crossed the platform and returned through Sox, Chinatown and Adams/Wabash to go partly round the Loop and then off west past factories and slums to trim Austin and another terminus at Harlem. Then back again to Clark/Lake, the iron forest of Lake Street, and spring sunshine catching the station's bright paint. O frabjous day! Relaxed indeed, we hoped that once a year at least the directors of the Chicago Transit Authority, in frock coats, top-hats and side-whiskers, ceremonially ride the 'L' while raising glasses of their best champagne to the World's Columbian Exposition of 1893 which gave it birth.

To realise what railways meant to the development of the American continent, go to Madison Avenue. There on the

Chicago, Madison Avenue station, 'the six stone columns . . . mighty in their upwards power'

corner of Canal Street stands the proud terminal, built in 1911, of the Chicago & North Western, the six stone columns of its Avenue frontage mighty in their upwards power. Inside, the marble pillars of the huge ticket hall sweep to a great curved roof, its span confidently decorated with motifs of railway wheels, bells, wrenches and hammers. All around were the polished wooden facades of brightly-lit shops, restaurants and snack bars (one with a fast track for extra-hurrying commuters). Beyond lies the concourse and the terminal's sixteen tracks. Madison Avenue is a *real* station.

There we took a diesel push-pull commuter train to Wheaton on the Geneva line, riding in an enormously high double-deck commuter 'streamliner' 144-seater in the CNW's green-and-yellow passenger livery. We had never been in such a huge coach. A central entrance vestibule gave on to two compartments, smoking one way, non-smoking the other, with ordinary seating each side of a central gangway; but also to staircases leading to each compartment's twin upper decks, each side having one row of reversible seats and a luggage rack over the gangways below.

English eyes collected details: few overbridges (and those well raised up) and many level crossings, thus enabling such lofty coaches to be used; instead of return tickets, two singles that could be used in either direction; a smart uniformed collector in each enormous coach to sell tickets from intermediate stations, these being then inserted in clips in front of the seats and at the side of the galleries to show who had paid; the regular announcements of the next station; and the freight cars of romantically-named railways, the Erie & Lackawanna, Soo Line, British Columbia, Norfolk & Western, Santa Fé, Union Pacific and Cotton Belt.

Chicago's Union station, built in 1924, has none of Madison Avenue's exuberance. Huge, with vast pillared portico and great shopping centre, it discreetly hides its trains. Maybe Union was built as a statement, a defiance of the motorcar and the road transport age that was by then well advanced.

'Draught beer' said the notice, so in we went. It wasn't good beer, but in the bar where we drank it we sat on wooden seats in a reproduction wooden railway coach with patterned iron luggage racks, ceiling light globes, and prints of old steam trains. At the next table the elderly woman with the bright red knitted coat and black lace hat, cigarette in mouth and stick swinging on the table top, might have come from east of London's Aldgate. Further along, comfortable in leather, solid with customers, is the Iron Horse Restaurant and Cocktail Bar. Inside, among the railway decorations, we saw a Southern Railway 'Platform 4' sign, and the board of The Railway Tavern, Ely Ales – maybe the souvenirs of some returning GI from World War II.

We still had to see that remarkably-named waterway, the Chicago Sanitary and Ship Canal. Late in the nineteenth century the city's death-rate from typhoid rocketed as more and more sewage poured into Lake Michigan only too close to the drinking water intakes. So, in January 1887, engineer Rudolph Hering proposed that the flow of the Chicago River should be reversed by blocking its exit with a lock, and then linking it with a deep cut forty miles long (fifteen miles being solid rock), to the Des Plaines River, which joined the Illinois, a tributary of the Mississippi. Thus Chicago's sewage would become someone else's problem, and simultaneously she would gain a modern waterway to replace the old Illinois & Michigan Canal.

So it was agreed. A new authority was set up, work began in 1892, and the new cut, together with a six-mile dredging of the Chicago River, was completed in 1900. Later, as the southern part of the city expanded, the same trouble began again, and was similarly solved, the Calumet River being reversed and led into the Sanitary Canal by means of the navigable Calumet–Sag channel.

Joliet, thirty-seven miles from Chicago, borders the ship canal, and thither we went on Amtrak's 'Inter-American' bound for St Louis, Missouri. Amtrak trains are named. So are many coaches; we picked *Angel Island, Loch Ness* and *Windy City* off one train, Windy City being Chicago's nickname. In the United States most railways remain privately-owned and more or less separate, but long-distance passenger services are worked by a national agency, Amtrak, their trains therefore running on company track.

We did a round trip to Joliet, out on the tracks of the Illinois Central Gulf, back on those of the Santa Fé. Outward-bound we paralleled the bed of the old Illinois & Michigan Canal for miles – much of it watered – and once saw a ruined lock with new stonework, as if preservationists had been at work. Emerging from Joliet station (huge waiting-room with wooden settles and a central iron radiator like a tortoise stove from some English cathedral) at speed, for we only had an hour between trains, we secured an ancient taxi and set off to see the ship canal. Fortunately the equally ancient driver had been in England during the war – indeed, in Charles's own Devon at Barnstaple, Croyde and Ilfracombe, and so, our brand of lunacy being quickly accepted as normal in Devon and perhaps also in Joliet, he entered into the spirit of canal-hunting.

Past an iron lifting-bridge over the canal, past a railway bridge whose central section rises vertically (what a paradise Chicago and its environs is for connoisseurs of iron bridges) past Joliet barge terminal, the superstructure of a towboat (push-tug) towering above tiers of barges, we came to Brandon lock, mitre-gated, huge, dropping the ship canal towards the Illinois River and faraway New Orleans.

In and out of the taxi for photographs, then back to Joliet to take a double-decker coach on the Santa Fé line, with splendid views of the ship canal and its traffic most of the way back. Very impressive, once past Lockport lock and Romeo, is the rock section, on one side of the rails the ship canal cut out of solid stone – if you doubt it, look at the quarries – on the other the smaller rock cut of the Illinois & Michigan Canal. Then into Chicago past industrial estates that line the canal for miles, good to see for those who seek to extend water transport. Our Amtrak tickets had had 'Welcome aboard Amtrak' on the front and 'Nice to have had you with us' on the back, and on our seats was a label 'Thanks for travelling with us'. To which we could only reply: 'Thanks for having us'.

So we returned to the familiar skyscrapers and to our last evening hotel coffee-house meal.

"Good-bye, you lovely people', said the cashier. 'Come back next year', said the dark-skinned waitress. Chicagoans unfriendly? Not they.

Next day we left Union station on the 'Cardinal' for our all-day journey slantwise across Indiana to Ohio's Queen City of Cincinnati, where we were to join the *Delta Queen*.

Amtrak is a curious mix. The 'Cardinal', in their nationwide red-and-blue livery, consisted of Budd-constructed stock with adjustable seats with leg-rests and individual tables; washrooms as well as men's and women's toilets, trash-cans (litter-bins) and a water tap with paper cups at the end of each car; a dinette or buffet car; and a train staff who could not have been smarter, nicer or more efficient. Our conductor was soon intimate with each of his passengers, kindly to some, ribbing to others, informative to all, telling us where we were, lifting people's luggage off the racks for them. Trains and staff are the nucleus of a fine railway service. All this was – certainly in the Chicago area, for we found it less so elsewhere – largely negated by the poor maintenance of the track and pointwork, which makes for a snail-like approach to and exit from terminals, and slow-running everywhere by British standards, to which is added such historical features as hair-raising right-angled railway level crossings and sharp curvatures. In no hurry, we enjoyed every minute of the eight hours it took to cover some 300 miles.

Past Calumet Harbour, over the Calumet navigable channel, a towboat glimpsed, and then another navigable channel to Indiana Harbour, with big ships on Lake Michigan's dark-green distances beyond, past great steelworks one after another we left Chicago for Indiana in early April; flattish, sandy soil changing to patches of black and then light loam, maize (corn) growing, with signs of spring only in the greening willow trees. Every hummock of high ground had its white-painted, wooden farm buildings, every view its silo, with here and there cattle, very occasionally sheep and pigs, and only once a glimpse of hens and ducks. We passed small neat towns of detached, mostly single-storey, green- or red-roofed wooden houses and countrified industry (Chew Mail Pouch Tobacco, ran one advertisement). All these were so neat, and yet there was so much litter – old cars, old junk, in a country whose size means that you don't have to clear up after yourself, but can always find another empty space.

We had been hoping for a glimpse of the derelict Wabash & Erie Canal, at 468 miles the world's longest. It was built in the last century across Indiana from Evansville on the lower Ohio to join the Miami & Erie, which ran from Cincinnati through to Toledo on Lake Erie. From Toledo mid-western wheat could be shipped to the east via the Erie Canal or the St Lawrence, and imported farm goods brought back. It therefore crossed Indiana on the opposite diagonal to our own railway. As we entered Peru station, there was Canal Street parallel to our track and, after we left it to swing right over the Wabash River, running straight ahead beside the stream was the raised towpath on the left, the canal's old bed to its right. We had seen and crossed it. And then our conductor told us that his wife's niece had lived in an old house nearby that had once been a canal hotel: it had a fireplace in every room, he said. That, we reflected, must have been quite something in the 1840s.

As we rolled south past Converse's County Fair ground where they were practising for harness (trotting) races, past Marion and Muncie, the green showed more and more on trees and bushes, with now the first ploughed fields. Climbing towards Richmond near the Ohio state border, the hills rose and an hour later we began a wonderful descent through them to Cincinnati by the river. One trestle viaduct after another, valley after valley, embankment after cutting, cutting after embankment, we cautiously caterpillared down to stop on the Ohio bridge, then, oddly, backed into Cincinnati's small village station. The fine old one, we were told, had been converted to other uses. We felt it an anticlimax in the dusk to trundle our suitcases on their little wheels over the bare tracks to an empty street. But the train's conductor ordered a taxi for us, and so sent us to dine, wine (Californian) and sleep.

On Sunday we walked down to the great Ohio River and the oldest bridge between the states of Ohio and Kentucky, opened in 1867, built by that prince of suspension-bridge engineers, John Augustus Roebling, the only man also to build suspension aqueducts for canals. And there, upstream, the *Delta Queen* was moored against the sloping bank, her gangway busy with little figures servicing her for us. Across river, about the width of the Thames at London, a twin-funnelled stern-wheeler, the *Mike Finch*, is now a restaurant. A towboat pushed eight loaded jumbos (a jumbo is a 1,500-ton barge) upstream, to be passed by a 15-barge tow three abreast of empty coal barges going down. Here was what we had come so far to see, the stern-wheelers and the towboats, the barges and the river: the waterways of America.

For tailpiece to this chapter we found, open on Sunday, the Old Wheel Café on Walnut Street near 6th. There, on a wall of pictures of old Cincinnati, were two of the Miami & Erie Canal before the Central Parkway was built where once canal water stood.

We had reached the river, been reminded of the canal: now for the *Delta Queen*.

Chapter 2

Delta Queen: Steamboat to New Orleans

As 6pm approached, the great red-painted stern-wheel began slowly to turn. Visitors went ashore, the ship's hooter blew long blasts, and the gangway swung up on its boom and round to its running position high above the bow.

Wheel now turning fast, the huge opposed cranks heaving up and down, the *Delta Queen* backed out into the Ohio and turned her head downstream, while at the two small keyboards of the calliope or steam organ (dating from 1897), Dan Forman played cheerful, but to us unrecognisable, tunes. Clouds of steam rose from the thirty-two shining gold-plated pipes of the moaning, whistling, gasping calliope; the noise was deafening; it was just the thing any steam enthusiast would want in his home. Those not watching Dan were drinking punch in the aft cabin-lounge: we were off on our 1,395-mile voyage to New Orleans, the only non-Americans among some 180 passengers.

Clouds of black smoke rose from the funnel and swelled upwards through the perforated decking of Roebling's bridge. The towers of Cincinnati fell behind, the towboat *Charleston* passed us pushing its eight jumbos heavily upstream, and we ran curving down between wooded hills and past tall, thin houses by a tall, thin church, reminiscent of the Danube between Passau and Vienna. But not for long. The *Queen* stopped, turned, and sheered over to a tank farm where for three hours she filled up with fuel oil.

Meanwhile the crowd of passengers was seriously engaged in sampling the first meal, a long buffet closely packed with meats, seafood, bright-coloured salads, vegetables and fruit and at the head of it the biggest joint of roast beef that we had ever seen, perfectly cooked pink and brown, being carved by a skilled man straight on to each plate. We faced the future with confidence.

'. . . the thirty-two shining gold-plated pipes of the moaning, whistling, gasping calliope'

After dinner we were introduced to Captain James Blum and his officers, one a woman. Tables were then cleared, the dining-saloon became the Orleans Room, and we listened to the southern jazz of Vic Tooker and the Riverboat Ramblers – trumpet, banjo, incredibly skilful percussion, double-bass (played by Vic Tooker's mother, a lively lady in her seventies) and piano. How many years rolled back as we once again found we couldn't 'give you anything but love, baby; that's the only thing I've plenty of, baby . . .'.

We slipped out early for a last walk round the deck to watch house lights twinkling high up among the dark woods, and to bed. In our bunks we drowsed to the sound we had not heard since we crossed Sweden on the Göta Canal in *Wilhelm Tham* in 1965, steam engines turning over. In our sleep we heard every now and then a single or a double hoot as she blew for port or starboard when she met upcoming tows.

To all appearances a typical Mississippi river-boat except for her single funnel instead of the usual two abreast, the four-decked *Delta Queen* has a curious history. Her hull was built at Isherwood's on the Clyde in 1926 and, with a stern-wheel shaft and cranks cast by Krupps, she and her then mate the *Delta King* were transported in knocked-down state to be reassembled and have their superstructures added in California. There they carried overnight passengers and cargo between San Francisco and Sacramento (the *Delta* of the vessels' names being that of the Sacramento, not the Mississippi River) until early in World War II; indeed, we found we had two passengers on board who had travelled on the *Queen* in those days. The dining-saloon, then the car-carrying deck, still has its original wooden floor. After a period in the US Navy ferrying troops in San Francisco Bay, the crated-up *Delta Queen* was towed by a tug through the Panama Canal to New Orleans in May 1947 to be rebuilt by Captain Tom Greene, whose father had operated steamboats out of Cincinnati since 1890. Since then she has changed hands more than once, till now she has The Coca Cola Bottling Corporation as financial backer, along with her newly-built sister, the *Mississippi Queen*. Her superstructure being wooden, she operates under a special Act of Congress which until November 1983 exempts her from the rule that no wooden ship may carry more than forty-nine passengers. The more unfortunate *King* became a lodging-house for Canadian lumberjacks; she still survives in very poor state in California, having been sold early in 1978, perhaps to become a floating restaurant.

From these odd origins the *Queen's* owners have created an opportunity for Americans to revisit their past. Her saloons are comfortable and spacious, her food good without being luxurious, her brass and polished-wood grand staircase giving just the right touch of grandeur. Her cabins are small, with cons only moderately mod. ('All mod cons' is an English house-agents' abbreviation for 'all modern conveniences', ie toilet and (probably) bathroom). There is no TV, no ship-to-shore telephones, no taped music and no juke-boxes; no stand for newspapers and magazines, but only *The Steamboat Times*, modestly described as 'The Western River's Greatest Daily Paper'. Once on board, time slips back fifty years or so, as the old stern-wheeler navigates the river at 9mph plus or minus the speed of the current.

The engine-room is a steam enthusiast's delight. Our shipboard friend Boyd Clapham, ex-US Navy, who owns and drives a 1919 Stanley steam car, took Charles down. The engines, designed and erected in California but built by Denny's of Dumbarton, are cross compound, with a high-pressure cylinder of 26in diameter and a low of 52in, each with a 10ft stroke. These are connected to two great pitman arms that run out to the cranks that turn the stern-wheel, each arm being 40ft long and weighing ten tons. The wheel itself, of wood except for the axle, hubs and strengthening bands, has a diameter of 28ft, width of 19ft, and weighs 44 tons. Four boilers, taken from a four-funnelled World War I destroyer, provide steam at 200–225psi working pressure while under way.

We woke to sunshine. It was not yet really warm, but passengers pretending it was smiled at Charles's duffel coat and cap – 'sailing North?' they grinned. We are still passing the hills of Indiana and Kentucky: their trees bright in spring's fresh green. By now our Englishness is common knowledge, and people come to tell us that their ancestors came from England, from Lancashire and Devon, Staffordshire and Lincoln. *The Steamboat Times* announces: 'International passengers joining us this cruise . . . Mr & Mrs Charles Hadfield of London, England'!!

After breakfast we pull into Louisville on the Kentucky shore of the Ohio. A bus tour goes ashore, but we stay put, for there is a limit to the new sights we can absorb. Beside us is the twin-funnelled *Belle of Louisville*, the oldest river-boat afloat, full of southern charm, and past the saloon windows go the great tows, ten, twelve, fourteen rigidly-lashed barges carrying oil, chemicals, sand and many unrecognised cargoes. They are pushed by huge towboats with crews of a dozen or more, their superstructures rising high to give their captains a clear view ahead of the tow.

The sun shone. The pale-blue sky was thinly flecked with clouds. We sat on deckchairs overlooking the stern-wheel's scarlet paddles, and for the first time this year felt hot in the open air. We should have left Louisville at 3pm, but didn't. Everything waited; warm in the sun, it didn't seem to matter. We just looked ahead to the patterned ironwork of the high girdered rail-bridge with a vertically-lifting span, whose operator has to ride up and down on the span in his little cabin. The bridge stands at the entrance to the short Louisville & Portland Canal, and we knew we'd get there sometime. To our right, where the river ran, the Falls of the Ohio once compelled all river cargoes to be unloaded above and below them, and portaged round. The enterprising citizens, who in 1830 opened the first by-pass canal with its three locks round the falls, found themselves with an instant commercial success, which three years later carried 1,585 boats of 170,000 tons capacity. Today, a much enlarged canal leads to the McAlpine lock with its single fall of 20ft (when we went through, for the fall varies with the amount of water in the river, and is normally nearer 25ft).

Eventually Wooten's River Service barge and towboat, the *Eleanor W.*, did come alongside, and did fill up our drinking-water tanks, and we did leave, to blow a long steam blast that echoed high away, and pass under the lift-bridge into the canal and to the 1100ft x 110ft lock built in 1963. To its left two chambers of the earlier canal's locks still stand. American river locks are mitre-gated (ie they swing sideways) unlike most on European rivers, which have vertically-rising gates and towering superstructures. We edged into the side, a hand on the end of the bridge chanting 'Six feet off, cap', 'Three feet off, cap'. Lock operation was fast and smooth, and soon we were out again on the broadening river to finish the day listening to 'Professor' Fred Dodd's feats on the banjo.

After breakfast Evansville, this time on the river's Indiana bank, the weather now warm enough for summer-weight clothes. We knew it as the southern terminus of the Wabash & Erie Canal we had glimpsed at Peru and, the *Queen* moored to the town's sloping hard, we set off to enquire about the canal at the brand-new Museum of Arts & Sciences. Instead, on a track outside, we found a 1908 steam locomotive originally built for the Chicago, Milwaukee, St Paul & Pacific Railroad, club car and caboose (guard's van), all put there by enthusiast effort, for America too has her railway buffs. Directed to the public library on Walnut Street and 5th, we were handed a historical folder and a town map. Comparison quickly showed the canal as having run past the library's front door. Entering the town along the line of the present Canal Street, it had turned sharply right along 5th, to end a few streets away just beyond the intersection with Vine Street.

There, by the Court House Center, was a plaque:

> Wabash & Erie Canal
>
> Completed from Lake Erie to Evansville, 1853. Used till 1865. Passing from 5th St to 1st Ave., canal widened into basin for docks covering part of this square.

Content with our achievement, we walked along Vine Street back to the *Queen*, past cherry, apple, lilac and dogwood all in bloom. Shirt-sleeved in the warm sun we saw swallows building along the river levee (flood embankment). On board the calliope was playing. Spring had come to Evansville, and over there, across a great curve of the Ohio, lay the South, whither we were bound.

A blast on the hooter, a fanfare on the calliope, and the *Queen* swung out to turn downstream. New Orleans, here we come – only a thousand miles to go, and above the bridge are the golden antlers that show our *Delta Queen* to be current winner of the annual river-boat race. In the Texas Lounge, Vic Tooker and the Ramblers burst into steamboat song: 'Sailing away, sailing away, on the *Henry Clay*'. Bright as buttons, middle-aged and elderly lined the lounge for southern songs, drinking whisky sours or long fruity drinks in tall iced glasses, clapping and beating time, finally scrambling to their feet to follow the trombonist round the room singing: 'When the saints come marching in'. We liked that.

Late that evening we came up from the Ramblers for the passage of Uniontown lock, the last of the trip. With only a few feet of fall, our lines were quickly cast off the floating bollards, and we rejoined the river past a waiting tow, flashing white light ahead, green starboard light, two white lights astern. Overhead, the three-quarter moon in a sky only wisped with cloud moved slowly across our bow as we took the bends. Every now and then one of our searchlights switched on and swung to pick up some mark on the bank, then off again in favour of the moon. Under the bridge there was no sound but a flapping halyard. Here for a moment was perfection.

America's quick-change weather hit us on Wednesday morning: a chill wind and grey sky instead of warmth and blue and small white horses on the green-yellow-grey of the water. No matter, for we were ahead of time thanks to a fast-running

The Delta Queen *at Cairo*

river, and a stop was arranged at Cairo (pronounced Cayro) on the Illinois bank a mile or so before the Mississippi River comes in from the north to join the Ohio. Cairo causes shipboard joking, perhaps because its small-town aspect contrasts so greatly with the two great rivers its neighbours; also because of its name, which is alleged to cause letters for *Delta Queen* passengers to finish up in Egypt.

Cairo is all right. Once you are through the hole in the high concrete levee wall stretching away in either direction that protects it from Ohio floods and past its self-confident notice: 'Welcome to historic Cairo, Gateway to the South', it offers pleasant countrified streets, with pretty pink or white wooden chapels and green or white wooden houses, a cinema, a local evening newspaper, Larry's Poodle Pad, a statue to *The Hewer* with a strong moral theme, and a huge post office within which a clerk pleasantly sold us airmail postcard stamps. Not a souvenir in sight.

The river at Cairo is a kind of marshalling yard. Here smaller barge-tows from the Ohio or the upper Mississippi are aggregated into tows of 40 or more barges for the lockless run to New Orleans. Similarly, upbound tows are split. So at Cairo there are always barges waiting, tows lined up to be dealt with; at one moment we got three towboats into one picture.

Off again, under a great road-bridge, and there, beyond a sandy point with a red marker, was the Mississippi itself, spanned by an even larger bridge. The ship's loudspeaker announced that here the muddy Ohio was about to meet the muddier Mississippi. There was indeed a line of colour difference, but not nearly as noticeable as, for instance, that between the Inn and the Danube at Passau. As we crossed the line, the big ship's bell at the bow was rung once. We had reached America's greatest river, if not particularly muddy, certainly wide – perhaps a mile here. Ashore the land is flat, the water fringed with smallish trees, the flood-line clear on bare trunks. Behind run the earthen levees that border the whole lower part of the river. Presumably towns and villages stand well back from such flood-endangered banks, for none appear.

We have searched the works of Dr Alex Comfort for a section

Towboat and tow on the Mississippi near Memphis

on 'sex and steamboating', or 'Joy in Confined Spaces'. There should be one. For a middle-priced *Delta Queen* cabin, its bottom bunk a little wider than the top and less than three feet clearance between the two, presents a challenge. No funny stuff, clearly. Fantasy is out. The pioneering spirit, the missionary approach, is required. Something as rugged as the bunks themselves – but steady, because of the hard shelves and harder bunk edges. Happily conscious of having just cleaned up $3.50 gambling on steamboat races in the Orleans room, we did fine. Others had to make do with less. When the pretty cabin maid directed Alice Mary to a tiny washroom stuffed with towels, tins of detergent and buckets, but provided with a big sink where she could wash some clothes, she found 'Louise's Love Nest' written on the door.

American cities have not got around to regarding a river as something their citizens might like to look at, even enjoy. Cincinnati and Louisville think the riverfront just the place for a motorway or two – so many indeed at Cincinnati that it is quite hair-raising to reach it. At Evansville and Cairo it has disappeared behind levees. And at Memphis, Tennessee, where we have now arrived, the locals consider that, because one wide road along the front might be lonely by itself, it should have a freight railroad as company. As we left our cabin for breakfast, a noise like an enraged mastodon arose, and two enormous diesels rumbled past, followed by the few dozen bogie-cars that make up a shorter American freight train. The stone-paved sloping river bank also makes a splendid overflow car park.

We first saw cotton at Memphis. Names of cotton factors lined the waterfront buildings and, two blocks inland, great bales piled the sidewalk, thick white wisps protruding. We also saw inner-city decay for the first time; empty streets, vacant lots, broken windows, derelict shops and a feeling of underlying passivity. Beale Street, once the home of the Blues, is part of it, though Schwab's extraordinary emporium survives, where one can buy anything from Gospel records to sunbonnets, along with its motto: 'If you can't find it at Schwab's, you're better off without it'.

Off again down the great river in the sunshine. We met barge-tows, coal, chemicals, gravel, sand and coal again, one tow with a Steermaster lashed at the head; it encloses bow-thruster power units to help turn the long tow round river bends. Then a coastguard craft changing buoys (in the States the word is pronounced beweys), to conform to a channel that never stays long in quite the same place. Islands come and go in the width of some three-quarters of a mile; beyond, trees and earth-banked levees stretch away to low hills. On the banks, the navigation markers shine, red to port, green to starboard as we run downstream. We are headed into a stiff wind: at the bow the house flag flaps madly; astern, passengers are trying their fingers on the calliope, and 'Yankee Doodle', 'Camptown Races' and 'Daisy Bell' float astern. The river opens up wide curve after wide curve; not conforming to these, the buoyed channel winds seemingly without reason across the water's expanse. On the bridge, a river pilot is always on duty, two of them working six-hour shifts.

The 300ft navigation channel is not, of course, there without reason; it is there because the US Army Corps of Engineers work to stabilise it by revetting (protecting with concrete mattresses) the river banks along critical sections, usually the outside of curves, and using dykes to close off secondary channels and reduce channel width, thus concentrating the river flow. Once stabilised, the Corps' dustpan dredgers – huge affairs that force strong jets of water on to the river bed, then push a huge dustpan along it to sweep up the loosened material – maintain the depth. But, the Mississippi being what it is, the channel doesn't always stay where it has been put.

Next morning, in sunshine but a cold wind, with some passengers doing 11-times-round-the-deck-makes-a-mile, we turned out of the Mississippi into the Yazoo River and, running between timber barges, came to the Vicksburg landing. Our fellow-passengers are fascinated, for Vicksburg was besieged for six weeks by General Grant during the Civil War, and when it fell, the Confederacy was split, the Mississippi was open to the Federal forces and the corn of the Middle West could once again find an outlet at New Orleans. Southerners reminisce. Northerners live the siege again. The Ramblers, seemingly Northerners to a man, defiantly play 'Back Home in Indiana' in the lounge, and sip Bloody Marys as they play.

Opposite the landing, on the high concrete levee wall, flood levels are painted, the first the most revealing, for in its few words lies the memory of an old disaster:

> 1927 if levees had held 62.7
> 1927 gage 58.4 as happen
> 1937 gage 55.5
> 1929 gage 55.2
> 1973 gage 53.5
> 1932 gage 51.9
> 1945 gage 49.8
> Courtesy of U.S. Army Engineer District, Vicksburg, Mississippi.

Vicksburg is a real 'sight', worth seeing not just for history, though it has plenty of that, but for good modern urban renewal. We began with the pre-Civil War Court House of 1858

Vicksburg: 'the Court House of 1858 with its jaunty cupola . . .'

with its jaunty cupola, perched high on a hill above the river valley and flanked by four little cistern houses where firefighting water could be collected. It is now a museum, in which one can see the intimacies of nineteenth-century life and the wreckage of the doomed Confederacy – its proclamations, postage stamps, uniforms and arms – amid splendid prints of the Federal fleet forcing the river passage and of Vicksburg's siege.

Then, with your tour guide to old houses, walk the shady streets and look at architecture amid azaleas until it is time to return past the syringa and the magnolia trees. As dusk fell, the *Delta Queen* pulled out, to run up the Yazoo River past the burnt remains of the *Sprague*, largest stern-wheeled steam towboat ever built, past the spot where the Federal gunboat *Cairo* went down (the first warship ever to be sunk by a mine) and the busy Vicksburg barge harbour, before turning back to seek the now moonlit Mississippi.

Saturday morning, fine and warm, found us running between cottonwood trees towards St Francisville. This is 'Ole Man River', immensely broad, deep, his current rippling, the number of barge-tows increasing – 'he jest keeps rollin' along'. Because he is too wide for many bridges, free car and passenger ferries operate: we moored alongside one at St Francisville.

Our idea of antebellum (before the Civil War) mansions having been derived from *Gone with the Wind*, we took tour coaches to Rosedown and The Myrtles. It was an extra that on our way we passed through St Francisville itself, a green-shaded white-and-yellow wooden-housed large village, and crossed the tracks of the West Feliciana Railroad. Proposed in 1830 as a carrier of cotton to the river, chartered in 1831 to run for 25 miles from Woodville to the now vanished port of Bayou Sara, its promoters differed from earlier railroad companies in first choosing the English or 4ft 8½in standard gauge, that of American railways today. Part was opened in 1840, the whole in 1842. The little railroad is still open for freight, the oldest stretch of the Illinois Central system, and we waved good wishes to it from the land whence railways came.

A line of white flowering shrubs marked the road front of Rosedown estate, and a simple pillared entrance turned into a long avenue under tall oaks cut to make a cathedral interior. As we walked up it a superb parkland estate opened on each side, at its centre a medium-sized simple dignified white country house. Two-storeyed in wood, with brick chimneys, dating from 1835, it stood a little high, wooden verandahs (terraces) on each storey, with rocking chairs in the shade and shutters to the rows of tall windows. Inside, it was a nest of small rooms, sitting-room, study, dining-room with punkah laid against the ceiling, butler's room giving access to the kitchen in a separate building (because of fire), children's dining-room, and a large bedroom specially built for Henry Clay, three times unsuccessful Presidential candidate, a man strongly in favour of preserving the Union and a friend of the owners, the Turnbulls. All were papered and furnished in an intimate, family style though with great wealth: French blue linen-paper wallpaper, rosewood and cypress bookcases, sewing tables, buffet, and four-poster beds with hand-embroidered covers. A smaller-than-baby-grand piano made by Chickering of Massachusetts stood in the rather crowded sitting-room.

Without elegant or grand entrance, steep black stairs led up almost directly from the hall door to a big landing, giving on to lighter, airy little bedrooms, here a zinc bathtub and rope to open the hatch above and tip the water, there a tall wide wickerwork drop-sided cot, three-wheeler push-chairs, dressing screens with glass uppers for sociability, and a landing niche filled by a tall birdcage. Imagination and beauty, showing in the details of the house, were opened and displayed in the ground surrounding it, where mystery of green shade and shapes of weathered statues under the moss-oaks alternated with rich or dainty brilliance, ponds, vistas and sunshine. A fanciful achievement was a tiny pavilion for two set between two ponds, each with exactly matching tall fountains, so that as you first saw it you exclaimed 'a reflection! a *trompe-oeil!*'. Then as the path brought you to a different angle you exclaimed: 'it's real, there *are* two fountains!'.

Grandeur and a sense of social life were well shown in the second house we saw, The Myrtles, which in its present form dates from about 1820. Long and low, with spreading gables, wooden terrace all round, and tall shuttered doors and windows, it opened onto a cool, big hall, a straight-sided staircase, and a series of big rooms all made to open out of each other for dances, parties and receptions. This house had been partly furnished and decorated by skilled foreign workmen brought over from Europe. Pierced plasterwork, *faux bois*, chinoiserie, Chippendale sets, delicate needlework decorated every room.

In either mansion, the mechanics of life were clear and practical given the Southern way of life – the cistern houses, outdoor kitchens, milk-shed, furnace, trough for skinning hogs – and three-holer wooden outhouse handy to the back door.

At breakfast-time on Sunday we came into New Orleans, which combines the romance of its French Quarter with being one of the world's great ports. To our left rose skyscrapers and the huge, low shape of the Sportsdome. Sunday or not, the river was alive with traffic: cargo vessels coming up from the sea to berth; push-tows; ferry-boats; tugs, all busily criss-crossing. LASH (Lighter Aboard Ship) barges lay at the Central Gulf Lines wharf, maybe destined to be lifted on board a barge-carrying ship for our own Thames. Hardly had we berthed before a refuelling tanker came alongside to replenish tanks before tomorrow's upriver journey.

On our last night on the *Delta Queen*, after listening once more to Vic Tooker and the Riverboat Ramblers, we sat on the top deck. On either riverside were spatters of lights, clustered here and there to show moored ships. The great road-bridge to our right was crowned with winking red lights and lined by the moving headlights of cars. And across, rising out of a patch of mist, was the full moon, so bright that each small cloud crossing her face made a brief dimness across the water. On such a night do travellers pause in thanksgiving.

New Orleans offers much, including a bus stop from which one may ride to Desire and Elysian Fields: maybe the one lies beyond the other. We were content to watch *Natchez*, another steam stern-wheeler, doing harbour trips, ride the single-decker streetcar along St Charles Avenue, and potter round the French Quarter. Our modest motor hotel was right in it, and the Mississippi Valley's oldest building, the Convent des Ursulines, was just down Chartres Street. We were delighted with the horse-headed metal posts along the pavement edges, perhaps once hitching posts, now protection from cars.

To a European, of course, the first thing that strikes one about the French Quarter is its familiarity: one has seen these narrow streets, these old painted houses whose iron grill gates offer glimpses of flowers and lawn, statuary and fountains, these open air cafes, this two- or three-storeyed trellised ironwork, this *place* with the church at one end and the market at the other, in a dozen French towns. Even the lettering of the Café du Monde is exactly French small town. But to ordinary Americans, who haven't been to Mexico or Europe, it must seem excitingly strange.

The French set it here in 1718, at the point where the Indians began their portage from the river to Lake Pontchartrain,

New Orleans, the French Quarter: '. . . this two- or three-storeyed trellised ironwork . . .'

naming it after the Duc d'Orleans, regent of France. In the next few decades they laid out the Vieux Carré, a grid of a dozen streets one way, fewer the other, on the riverbank as it is now. A treaty then ceded it to Spain, and from 1762 to 1803 the streets bore Spanish names (they still do, side by side with French), and more buildings appeared, not very different. It then became Napoleon's, but only for long enough for him to sell it the same year to the United States in the transaction called The Louisiana Purchase.

Here, in the French Quarter, we do as we would in France: stroll in the morning, sit in the open air for a coffee or a chocolate, buy a newspaper, decide on a little place for lunch, look at a sight or two; then an afternoon siesta in our cool, dark windowless air-conditioned room in a long, low hotel, a swim in the pool below; and then another stroll that will end with a meal, a bottle of wine, and a walk back beneath the gas jets and the moon.

By ignoring all the recommended restaurants of the guide books, and using our European eyes, we quickly found Ruggiero's in Decatur Street near Dumaine, and there every evening we ate and drank cheaply and well: good Italian cooking applied to New Orleans seafoods as to Italian veal parmesan or scallopine, and homely Valpolicella. When one evening Alice Mary asked for cheese, which does not appear as a separate end-of-meal item on American menus, our motherly waitress produced three Italian varieties especially for us from some private proprietorial store.

Below Jackson Square, that was once the Place d'Armes and then the Plaza de Armas, and is now centred on a spirited equestrian statue of Andrew Jackson (it makes a splendid perching place for pigeons), a plaque commemorates Nicholas Roosevelt, who captained the first steamboat to reach New Orleans from the Ohio on 10 January 1812. There lay the beginning, not of the French Quarter, but of the great modern city and port, with its 80 miles of wharves; there, where the sea met the river, where steam hauling cargoes down the rivers met steam hauling cargoes across the oceans. Here in Chartres Street is France, Spain, France again; but there, over the levee wall, is America.

Charles has always loved trams from the days of boyhood rides on the reserved-tracked, railway-railed Johannesburg trams that ran to Orange Grove and Norwood. There is nothing like a ride on public transport for seeing cities and other people. It was so on the Elevated in Chicago, it was to be so again on the St Charles Avenue streetcar line. (In the French Quarter, as we set out, we noticed some old iron plates in the sidewalk stamped 'Dept des Flambeaux et du Gumbo'. When we had had gumbo soup the night before we hadn't known what gumbo meant. We knew now.)

Only one streetcar line remains in New Orleans, the eight miles from Canal Street along St Charles and Carrollton

Avenues, a bargain at 30 cents fixed fare (have the money ready, for no change is given). For those who had almost forgotten the electric tram's warning 'ting-ting', the single-decker olive green workmanlike cars with overhead trolleys were nostalgic. But the line is not just for tourists: except for one other couple, the packed customers were locals.

Beginning in business streets, after Lee Circle the line enters a grass-covered, central reserved track, changing also from tram-type to railway-type rails. Old Lafayette Square and the area of city government left behind, you pass through 'small business' streets, and gradually come into tree-shaded areas of big houses, increasingly splendid, even fantastic, of the wealthy nineteenth century, with classical porticoes and pillars, or Victorian magnificence of turret and roof-spread. Then the modern world begins, a hospital, school buses, the Universities of Loyola and Tulane, synagogues, quantities of churches of known and curious denominations, then blocks of smaller housing, garages and shops. We see splendid street names like Harmony, Terpsichore and Constantinople. People board or leave the car at every stop. The journey reaches right out past Audubon Park and Zoo to its Carrollton Avenue end. Returning, we notice that each house stands alone in its own little or big patch of ground: there are no terraces. In the French Quarter each garden is surrounded by its house as a patio or court, and life is lived within, or on the sidewalks; but up St Charles Avenue people move outwards as the world has done since the nineteenth century.

New Orleans is a river, but also a canal, city. She does not in the least resemble Venice to look at, but many an ancient Doge must from his heavenly gondola be approving that application of business acumen to a superb waterway site that has made New Orleans, as it once made Venice, a great city and port. She stands not only on the Mississippi, but at the centre of canals that join her and the river to the Gulf Intracoastal Waterway, opened in 1945, the protected line of busy water that runs in one direction to Florida, in the other almost to Mexico. Westwards the old Harvey Canal and much newer Algiers Canal leave the Mississippi separately through entrance locks, one each side of the greater New Orleans highway bridge, but soon coalesce on their way to the Intracoastal's western section. On the opposite (left) bank, the Inner Harbor Navigation Canal takes off, to become the Mississippi-Gulf outlet, New Orleans' link with the eastern Intracoastal.

Yet . . . as we stood on Canal Street, that tremendous boulevard that runs inwards from the river towards Lake Pontchartrain, we made the mistake many must have made before: 'Obviously, a filled-in canal'. Not so. Back in Spanish days, governor Carondelet had made a little canal from Lake Pontchartrain, five miles away behind the city, to the ramparts at the edge of the French Quarter. In 1807 Congress enacted that the city should reserve space for a canal to continue Carondelet's work to the Mississippi, and for warehouses alongside. The Orleans Navigation Company never built it, and when in 1852 the company was wound up, the reserved land became Canal Street, its great width of 171ft commemorating the reserved canal track of 50ft and two 60ft side reservations.

On our last day we climbed the levee wall for one more look at the spreading river port that had already become familiar, then visited the Mississippi rooms of the Cabildo museum at Jackson Square to see its many steamboat pictures, then paid a last visit to Canal Street that should have been a canal.

Standing that night, after a late bathe, on our hotel balcony above the swimming pool, we watched a procession of portly American males filling plastic buckets from the ice machine. It was as pleasantly warm as an English summer evening, and later, by turning off the air-conditioning and getting under a coverlet as well as a blanket, we were to sleep soundly. Why the ice, we wondered, as we had wondered at the American way of serving iced water at the beginning of all meals; at breakfast iced water and hot coffee arrive simultaneously. Thereupon we evolved a theory for which we are sure there is no medical foundation. By using so much ice Americans artificially lower their body temperatures. Then they have to eat large meals, in which fries, egg dishes and bread are prominent, to replace this lost body heat. Hence the weight problems that are widely shared by men and women, white and coloured alike. The solution – ban all ice machines. Having satisfactorily settled that one, we went to bed. Tomorrow we were to fly east and south to West Palm Beach in the south of Florida, there to join the *New Shoreham* on a two-week's voyage up the Atlantic Intracoastal Waterway to Rhode Island.

Chapter 3

Florida to Rhode Island in *New Shoreham*

Our plane from New Orleans for some way flew along the Gulf Intracoastal's channel beside the sea; tiny as matchboxes, towboats were guiding their precedent barges. An hour later, as we curved down to West Palm Beach, another towboat was guiding other barges on the Atlantic Intracoastal, usually called the Inland Waterway, lying behind the seafront buildings of Palm Beach. This line of lagoons, rivers, bays, canals and short stretches of sea extending from southern Florida to New England was to companion us for 1,717 miles and 14 days to Warren, Rhode Island.

Punctually at 9 am on Sunday 30 April, the 125ft long *New Shoreham* backed out of the port of Palm Beach and turned north. On board were 65 passengers, 62 of them American, one Canadian, and two English. On either bank high blocks of flats gave way to single-storey winter houses, cool behind arched verandahs, and fronted by palms and tropical trees. Speedboats cavorted round and past us, and every mile or two we blew for a road-bridge to lift or swing, then again blew our thanks. We were waved to, and waved. Once we grounded gently, then slid off – and memories of English canals came crowding in. Then houses too fell away, and green banks backed by yellow pines fringed the waterway. Enticing little creeks opened, and patches of white sand showed along the banks. Marinas appeared and were left behind: cruisers, yachts, speedboats, water-skiers, fishermen, passed us. We saw our first pelicans, brown and white, two on the water and one flying.

Waterway cruising, we reflect, is surely one of the major pleasures of life. We sit in the forward lounge, orange drink in hand. The banks slide past the windows, always changing, always showing something new, different, odd. Ahead stretches the water, rippled, cloud-reflecting, broken now and then by the passing craft of the potterers, the speed boys, the families, the show-offs, the cruiser-fishermen, rods vertical on each side of their cabins. On the left red, on the right green, markers show the dredged 400ft channel. Roots of mangrove trees twine in the water; Norfolk palms, fruiting orange trees, hibiscus and bougainvillea pass by; a cormorant sits on a post. Two passengers start getting their exercise by walking round the deck. A flock of two dozen pelicans sits on a passing sandbank, and Alice Mary hopes for an alligator. Maybe it is the S-bend of a pelican's neck that persuades us he is such an agreeable bird. Bridges lift as we approach: lines of cars form on each side, then disperse. The temperature is in the mid-70's, with sunshine bright in a heavily clouded sky, and a cool breeze. Approaching cruisers come close to look at us. Above Stuart the boats die away: without the trees it could almost be the Mississippi. Tiny islands appear, with bunches of trees and bay-grape bushes huddled on exiguous sand. We overtake a yacht with a Red Ensign, from Tortola, British Virgin Islands. At the water's edge men are scooping clams and mussels.

The *New Shoreham* was a modern, twin-screw, twin-ruddered craft operated out of Warren, Rhode Island, by American-Canadian Line. She was powered by two General Motors 12-cylinder diesel units: two GM 6-cylinder motors drove her generators, with a 4-cylinder British-built Bedford as standby. Carrying some 66 passengers, she had small but perfectly adequate accommodation and provided plain, well cooked and plentiful meals to a fixed menu. We liked the custom of having no fixed seating in the dining-saloon, so that one could circulate among the other passengers; the ship's library of books and magazines; the saloon piano; and the all-day help-yourself service of coffee and soft drinks. Unlike *Delta Queen*, she moored up most nights.

At 5pm drinks were set up in the lounge for the captain's party, everyone helping themselves as long as the supply lasted. Tall, handsome, thirty-year old Captain Bob Whittaker, in pink shirt and brown trousers (uniforms were not worn on *New*

Shoreham) gravely circulated. Then a quick tidy-up before dinner at six.

That night, at Eau Gallie just above Melbourne, in an orange sunset we anchored, the only time we did so, and swung gently to the wind till an early morning start. We breakfasted to the sight of the huge rocket storage building at Cape Canaveral, a sky-pointing silo beside it, while porpoises frisked beneath our bows.

At a swing-bridge a Floridian called:

'Where are you for?'

'Rhode Island', we chorused.

'Why?'

Ahead, the narrow buoyed channel winds across a lagoon whose banks are only just visible; our wash, breaking outside the buoys, shows its narrowness. An extrovert cruiser overtakes us, so close as almost to shake hands, then cuts sharply in front of us to disappear up the narrow channel. Soon we turn sharply to the right, aiming to cut through the bank by the grove of orange trees that separates Indian River from Mosquito Lagoon. The lagoon narrows to a channel between low banks, backed by thin pines and tough palms reflected deep into the water. Groups of houses appear, on creeks or the main line; men sit on outboards, fishing; a crabber follows his line of coloured buoys, hauling up his catches. Ahead, high buildings show on the Atlantic side: Daytona Beach on whose hard sand Sir Henry Segrave and Sir Malcolm Campbell both set up world land speed records. Pelicans line a sandbank to port as a bridge rises for us; slim egrets, pure brilliant white, crested, opening wide wings, stalk on a sandy island; butterflies and long black dragonflies flutter over our deck; a yacht from Maine passes us going south. All this is Florida: warm, cheap retirement country where, with a plot and a boat, many find happiness.

Marineland is a marina, but also a research centre of the University of Florida. *New Shoreham* tied up there among the sea-going cruisers with their driving positions high above the cabins; one showed a certificate with 'Courtesy Examination, 1978'. The storm arrived soon after we did. Rain rattled down,

New Shoreham *at Marineland*

lightning flickered under heavy black clouds. Then, suddenly, the sun broke through the wet black in a misty, blazing ball of orange, its colour spread under the sky's dark ceiling and against the palmettos along the shore; within half an hour the commotion had gone and all was quiet again. Next morning we walked over to the sea and bathed. Great sweeps of fine sand, lines of rock dividing the beaches, a faint mist over the warm water and light cloud veiling the sun. Over there was England. We were comfortably cool watching the smooth low rollers lazily breaking, and a little wading bird strolling on thin legs.

The heavy riverbank vegetation we had found south of Marineland now gave way to low banks and swampy stretches as we entered the Matanzas River on our approach to historic St Augustine. We noticed its differentness before we reached it, for instead of steel its bridge was mainly of concrete, a central lifting span between four little red-roofed towers.

Don Juan Ponce de Leon (his statue stands by St Augustine's Plaza) had sailed with Columbus's second expedition in 1493. Based thereafter in the New World, he equipped his own expedition to explore to the north, and in April 1513 made landfall near here. It being the Easter season – *pascua florida* in Spanish – he named his discovery La Florida, and claimed it for Spain. Fifty-two years later, on 8 September 1565, Captain General Pedro Menendez de Aviles established here, on land easily accessible to, yet sheltered from, the sea, the first permanent settlement in North America. Thus the locals claim St Augustine as America's oldest town and first Christian parish.

It is, of course, a tourist place. Its motels, rubber-tyred road trains and souvenir shops show that. But the tourism is not obtrusive. We found St Augustine friendly and interesting, and liked it. Much seems to be owed to the work over many decades of the local Historical Society's efforts to research the town's past, restore old buildings, and give the place a sense of identity.

We made straight for the castle. One doesn't expect castles on American soil, but this was a real, solid, stone, star-shaped, moated, drawbridged, cannon-supplied castle: at least, the Spanish called it *castillo*, and we prefer that to 'fort'. Begun about 1672, worked on for many decades thereafter, it was successfully defended against more than one British attack. Transferred with all Florida to Britain in 1763 in exchange for Havana, it became Spanish again in 1783, and finally American in 1813. Its troops' quarters have seen the flags of four states – Spain, Britain, the United States and, briefly, the Confederacy. They still fly throughout the town, the British flag that from before 1800, without the St Patrick's cross.

Having climbed over and round the castle, we pottered through the little town with its pleasant tree-shaded semi-tropical pinkish streets and squares with glimpses of green, flowered, patioed gardens scented with magnolia or jasmine, to the 'Oldest House'. It has been called the oldest in the USA; the oldest Spanish house in the USA; but wisely, it is now officially just the 'Oldest House', and charming it is, standing cool in its

St Augustine: the 'Oldest House', standing cool in its tropical patio garden

tropical patio garden. The lower walls of the two-storeyed building are of old Spanish construction: coquina, a natural shellstone found across the bay at Anastasia Island, set on a foundation of oystershell. The lower floors are tapia – a form of concrete made from burned oystershell, lime and sand. Inside, the furniture represents those who have lived here – Spanish, British, Spanish again, American; we took pleasure in a grandfather clock with a Swaffham, Norfolk, name on its dial. And the British put in the fireplaces.

America passes by. Snug houses in clearings; wide marshes; the silhouette of a distant aircraft carrier at Maryport below Jacksonville; four big motor-cruisers coming up astern and passing. They are from New Jersey, Toronto, Ohio and North

Carolina, such is the spread of waterways. A huge pipe assembly on several barges trails by, with a tug ahead and three others helping – part of a dredging outfit being moved, for here, where the waterways are so wide, material dredged from the channel is pumped ashore, surplus water then being allowed to run back. Egrets and white herons ornament the marshy banks. Buffet lunch appears on deck as we pass Fernandina Beach and its lines of moored shrimping-boats. Across the St Mary's River and we are in Georgia.

We moor at St Simon's Island, Georgia, one of the twelve Golden Isles, seawards of the main Intracoastal channel, and find the answer to one of those unformulated questions one carries with one through the years. For here, part of St Simon's Island, is Sea Island, whence was named a special strain of long-staple cotton. In fact, the Civil War ruined the island's cotton-growing economy, but the old name still lives on many a shirt label.

The pier, occupied by men and boys catching catfish, lies by the village. A short walk yields a lighthouse built in 1872, a secondhand bookshop where we bought *Alice in Wonderland*, wide-spreading holm-oaks shading picnic seats, palm trees, swallows and jackdaws, a dark-brown squirrel, flower-beds bright with antirrhinums, pinks, sweet williams, marigolds, azaleas and bottle-brush bushes and, up a side lane, sheets of wild honeysuckle climbing over hedge, bush and tree. In the neat village street we chuckled at 'The Laziest Shop in Town'. As we walked slowly back to *New Shoreham*, a shrimping-boat motored quickly past, a crowd of gulls following.

Two or three miles away is Fort Frederica, first established here by the English in 1736 as part of a policy of containment of the Spanish, said to be then their biggest fortification in the New World. With James Oglethorpe, who founded it, were John and Charles Wesley, then Church of England ministers, who preached under a tree to soldiers and townspeople before Christ Church was built at the fortified settlement. So, moored to St Simon's Island pier, we are linked with Hymns Ancient and Modern as with the shirt-shops of Jermyn Street.

How nice Americans are! Our interest in canals and

waterways is now well known throughout the boat, and several people enquire about voyaging on English canals, on the Rhine, Danube, Göta Canal or French waterways. We are becoming pundits, writing addresses, giving advice. The two or three canal books in the ship's library are being searched so that readers can keep their ends up when talking to us. More, we have been told of cousins in East Grinstead, aunts in Tring; of visits to London, Devon, Dorset, Scotland; of ancestors from Yorkshire, Cheshire, Staffordshire. Friends living nearby are brought on board at overnight stops to be introduced to us – we guess just to listen to our English voices. Even if sometimes we feel a little like deer at a zoo, no one could be other than grateful for the kindliness and goodheartedness with which buns are offered, and noses stroked.

'A talk from the Cook' went up on the noticeboard. Stage props were blackboard, chalk and duster; curtains rose as the kitchen door into the dining-saloon was flung open and out leapt the star, our lanky dark-eyed Bob. He was shouting before his hand reached the blackboard chalk: 'I'm going to tell you about cooking, you may all be good cooks but I was trained to it six years – it's hard work if you're going to be good, and you all have got to be good. I'm good too, and I'm going to tell you what I know is the basis of being good. Now – soups first and that means stock – broth, consommé, bouillon, cream, bisque – they all want stock. *So*' – he drew his first breath and flourished their names on the board while his talk poured on. He whirled through 'pea soup 1 quart chicken stock 4 ounces yellow split peas boil till obliterated, cup of fat and cup of flour for roux, mix and add to milk etc and heat, for thick soup add ground beef must be ground beef –' he swept pea soup and roux off the board – 'in adding roux always remember to heat it before adding to your stock or it'll go lumpy'. The dark eyes gripped us as he cried: 'Always remember that, hot to hot, cold to cold, or you can throw it in the garbage'. We shrank, and he stormed on – 'eggs, separate yolk from white through hand, *always hand*, don't freeze, omelettes, custard, frying, lard; coffee, biscuit, pancakes, rice any, questions?' Acceleration through all the vegetables, mayonnaise, sweet relish, to crust, cookies, 'don't mess about with bowls, put everything in one bowl and mix it all together, any questions?' – here I gasped 'Yes, please, how much is a cup?'. 'Eight ounces' was out with a kindly gleam, and we were away on puddings, icings, meringues – 'any heat's too hot, cook with portable torch' – frozen puddings, cream, 'never re-freeze or you can throw it in the garbage, never forget, cold to cold, hot to hot, any questions?' It was the fastest moving evening of the cruise, and assuredly I will 'never forget'. Later, in acknowledgement of our Englishness, Bob presented us with a bottle of Worcestershire sauce.

Approaching the Savannah River, the channel winds behind sheltered islands and then across sea sounds where the wind catches us and white horses slap our sides. This is marshland backed by trees, and miles have passed since we last saw a house. Cruisers come and go, northward bound for New York or Canada, and occasionally a tug hauls a line of pontoons or a maze of pipework. We motored gently all day, under the blue sky and the bright sun. On each side the flat marsh or grassy land stretches away, patches of blue-green or reddish colour suggesting reeds, the scarce trees much battered by wind or by water sucking the soil away from their roots. It was desolate, yes, but grand in its huge scale and sky, and shot with white or orange flash of birds, fishing-boats' rusty nets, red shirts in blue outboards threading a channel. Behind islands, across sounds, along rivers, past Thunderbolt with its shrimping-boats and marinas, past the Savannah River that divides Georgia from South Carolina, past Beaufort with the red sun sinking, a glow on the water ahead and a shapely wake falling astern, to beautiful Charleston promontoried between the Ashley and Cooper Rivers, gazing seawards past Fort Sumter where the Confederates fired the first shots of the Civil War in 1861.

How can the English understand what these southern Americans feel about the Civil War or, as it is more often called down here, the War between the States? In Charleston we saw our first Confederate war memorial to men 'who gave their lives for their country'. Every scrap of Confederate history is remembered and preserved, and yet one detects widespread relief that the Confederacy went so soon after it came.

Discussing this point with an informed American friend that evening, he produced a statistic (which we afterwards had confirmed by others) to illustrate how deep the Civil War goes in national consciousness; that twice as many American men lost their lives in it as in all the other wars together that America has fought from the 1776 Revolutionary War to Vietnam, including both World Wars. There could therefore have been few families in the north, almost none in the south, who had not lost at least one member in it. Gettysburg alone, he said, took more lives than did all Vietnam. Certainly, as we continued to travel, our impression strengthened that the Civil War means far more to Americans than the Revolutionary or indeed any other war except perhaps Vietnam: those two alone have gone deep into the national consciousness.

Old Charleston, roughly south of Calhoun, east of Coming and Logan Streets, is a place to stroll in. Mostly from 1800, simple, small, balconied wooden houses in many colours give place to bigger and yet bigger buildings, many fronted with the white house-high pillars that nineteenth-century Americans reckoned gave credibility to their achievements. Beautiful decorative details are lavished on main windows and porches. All shapes and sizes, almost all charming, the painted houses front narrow, tree-shaded streets, and between them are glimpses of lawns, roses, pools and rocking-chairs. Our noses twitched with passing scents.

St Philip's Church stands in Church Street, the first building on the site dating from about 1690. This, the third, was begun in 1835. English eyes will slide past the plaque commemorating the two signers of the Declaration of Independence who lie buried in the churchyard, to the cool interior with white-painted box pews, bordering galleries, and deep semi-circular sanctuary. Sit there, and join those earnest men and women who, a hundred and twenty years ago, must have prayed long and with agony – potential Confederates upon whether to break with the Union alongside Federalists upon how best to preserve it.

We had only hours in Charleston; we would have wished for days. Especially we should have liked to see the museum of the

Charleston: St Philip's church and, on left, the old theatre

Railway Historical Society, and pay our respects to the first steam-hauled railway in the United States, along whose six miles of track passenger trains, hauled by the American-built 'Best Friend of Charleston', began to run on Christmas Day 1830. By October 1833 the whole length of 136 miles had been completed to Hamburg, the world's longest railway at that time.

As we left our moorings, a pelican joined the rush of gulls to the galley windows. He caught some bits but couldn't keep pace with the gulls, fell behind, and plumped down on the water. Moving north up the Intracoastal, we realised that it was Saturday afternoon: cruisers, water-skiers, water-scooters frisked about us, happily risking suicide under our bows should an engine cut out. All were agreed on one thing, that the good speed was full speed. On deck we ate a buffet lunch, languidly waving our forks at brown bodies that rushed past between two upflung waves.

The evening was perfect. Gleaming, still water ahead reflected every passing beauty. *New Shoreham* wound through the Waccamaw River's woods, where egrets nest in dead trees or on the navigation's marker posts, and woodpeckers tap on each side. Warm, we sat on deck as darkness fell, the bow spot-lights came on, and a lookout was posted. Curve after curve, red light to port, white on its green marker to starboard, sky full of stars, until clustered lights showed ahead, and we came in to moor at Buckport's marina. A row of lighted boats, a restaurant, a grocery and hardware shop still open at 9.30 on a Saturday evening. Beyond, woods and darkness under the stars. As we went ashore, there arose that nostalgically familiar sound of crickets chirping that everyone born in Africa, like Charles, has always in his ears. The air was sweet with honeysuckle, and down a side track a bullfrog spoke. Next morning a long wooded artificial cut took us back towards the sea at the border with North Carolina.

That night we brought out the Mateus Rosé we had bought at the liquor store at St Simon's Island, chilled it in the ice-box, and drank it at dinner out of cabin tooth-mugs. American drinking customs seemed as odd to us as ours must be to them. The boat has no licence to sell liquor; too many state boundaries, each with its own laws, for that. So passengers bring their own bourbon and scotch, gin and vodka, and mix themselves cocktails (a word current here, dated with us). But drinking at meals, whether wine as now or occasionally a tin of beer, was confined to us. We were to find it general that Americans and Canadians appear seldom to drink with meals, except in the more expensive restaurants and hotels, and then only occasionally. Only Californians from their own wine-growing areas were exceptions.

Ashore, saloons look forbidding. One peers into the semi-darkness, to see the customers huddled at tables, or in a long line at the bar silently watching colour television. Liquor shops take some finding; when found, they carry a far higher proportion of spirits, and lower of wine and beer, than an English off-licence. American beer is always lager, almost tasteless, invariably over-chilled. Americans think it great. Canadian, we were to discover, is better. Twice we have seen Guinness advertised, once Bass . . . We do miss English beer in English pubs:

> 'O Beer! O Hodgson, Guinness, Allsopp, Bass!
> Names that should be on every infant's tongue!'

Next morning, Sunday, most of us gathered in the saloon for as informal a Sunday service as we had ever experienced. Céline gave out the hymns, the coloured Bahamian girls from the galley provided the choir, and added two hymns of their own composition, and the captain offered an impromptu prayer. It was offered sincerely, and by some, perhaps most, received sincerely; and as Christians ourselves, it spoke to our condition.

Here let us introduce Céline, officially purser: not young, not beautiful, but with a personality in a thousand. When not handing round hymnbooks she was responsible for replenishing the ship's stores. Before mooring stops, she put up leaflets about the places we were coming to, then arranged our tours. She sold stamps for postcards, posted the mail at each stop, and kept stock of things to buck you up or calm you down or prevent you feeling seasick or open your bowels or shut them. If a button came off, Céline had needle and thread; if one needed a safety-pin she provided it.

But she was more than all these. She was the confidante and support of half the passengers and all the crew. As we used to descend the companionway to the saloon, there Céline would be sitting, gaze concentrated on some elderly passenger's face, listening to the details of the latest grandchild, difficult son, husband's success, plans for retirement. Not half-heartedly, nor in the 'how soon can I get away' fashion, but with sincerity and human feeling. She was a real person.

We spent the next night at Wrightsville Marina. These American marinas are impressive: fuel supplies, plug-in electricity metered to each boat; shop, restaurant, showers and, here, covered moorings able to take those large, expensive sea-going cruisers that have a towering series of superstructures built for deep-sea fishing. Boats – fast boats, luxurious boats, boats equipped for fishing – are, one guesses, currently much more status symbols, examples of what Thorstein Veblen called conspicuous consumption, than are cars, now these are too pervasive to be exceptional. Status symbols or not – and which of us can really do without status? – they are lovely craft, and such marinas as Wrightsville care for them well.

Past Swanboro, and the character of the Inland Waterway begins to change. Up to now most of its course has been by lagoons, rivers and artificial cuts running just inland from the sea. But here a thin slice of land takes off north-easterly into the sea to become Cape Hatteras, then run north-westerly past the Wright Brothers' Kitty Hawk to rejoin the land mass near Norfolk at the entrance to Chesapeake Bay. Soon, at Beaufort, we shall turn to port into the Adams Creek Canal and, well within the barrier all the way, navigate to Norfolk, Virginia, where it ends, by canals, estuaries and sounds, a winding, varied route that includes some of the oldest artificial sections of the Waterway. We are a little sad, however, that at the approach to Norfolk, where there are alternative routes, we are to take the Albemarle & Chesapeake Canal and not its alternative, the Dismal Swamp. The latter is old and historic: George Washington, who was concerned with as many American enterprises as Queen Elizabeth slept in English beds, helped to initiate it. More, we had its written history on our shelves at home. However, what is one disappointment among so many pleasures?

Under grey clouds and in light mist we crossed Pamlico Sound, cut past little Hobucken with its moored fishing-boats, and set out across the Pamlico River on our way to Belhaven which, a notice on our board tells us, has 2,000 people and 16 places of worship. Land dies away in the mist, then reappears:

a brown pelican flies past among the seagulls. We pass a fishing-boat, net-booms out at an angle each side and astern, squatting like a huge bird on the water.

We like American small towns. A marina on one creek, on another fishing-boats moored beside the Belhaven Fish & Oyster Co (Crabmeat, Shrimp and Crab Meal), from which a strong smell of fish invigorates the patients in the hospital across the creek. The main street has one set of traffic lights (a sign of municipal adulthood that we've noticed before), and its wide shop-bordered length carries the injunction: 'No Parking at any Time'. We peered into the brightly-lit interior of the Wachovia Bank & Trust Co. On the back wall was a perfectly enormous safe, hung with wheels and dials, and in full view of the street. It's as secure a way as any of keeping the cash, we supposed, though we did wonder whether it was for show, the specie being really kept in a cupboard in the basement.

The absence of garden fences gives side streets a great impression of width: lawns run to the pavement edge, trees overhang it, some as enormous as the willow oak that must have greeted Belhaven's first inhabitants. Each brightly painted wooden house stands alone, most with comfortable front verandahs, and on them a couple of rocking-chairs, his and hers. Theft is no problem here: children's bicycles lie where they have been dropped, and in the main street a shop had not bothered to take in overnight its display of pot plants and fertilisers. America has a serious major crime problem, but it seems to be remarkably free from petty larceny and indiscriminate vandalism. The result, probably, of a tougher police approach.

That night the crew entertained the passengers in a show as hilarious as it was unsophisticated. The Bahamian girls sang and danced; the captain told funny stories; a deckhand recited; and Bob the cook of our gripping lecture, in short skirts and flowing hair, told quick-fire stories with action. It ended with a crew and passenger rendering of the hokey-pokey, and much swapping of stories afterwards in the lounge.

We woke to the tree-bordered banks of the 20-mile Alligator River–Pungo River Canal, and breakfasted to its debouchment into the Alligator. Rivers run larger than the simple English expect. Here we are moving down the river towards Albemarle Sound; at least, so the chart tells us, but in the light mist both banks are dim shapes in the distance. Not a boat is in sight, and to all appearances Europe lies ahead. However, a bridge appears, and we are reassured. It is quite enormous, for we count over 100 spans, and the end fades into the mist.

One has only to listen to the passengers to realise the size of the United States, and the perpetual curiosity of one part about the other. We have a rancher from Washington state and a printer from California; steel men, compressor men and insurance men, New Yorkers and Floridians and a captain from Maine. Quick-fire questions, quick-fire jokes, no offence taken or given in either, and a boat-wide feeling of responsibility that the English should be made to feel welcome. At the same time, a certain amount of awe that we both write books makes itself felt. It reminds us a little of Thurber's Mrs Munroe, meeting her husband off an ocean-liner: as soon as she saw him from the dockside standing on the upper deck, she knew that he had been reading a book.

By the afternoon, Albemarle Sound behind us, we had come up the North Landing River to the Albemarle & Chesapeake Canal that leads to the Elizabeth River, Norfolk, and Chesapeake Bay. It was originally built by a canal company in 1859, with one lock at Great Bridge to prevent salt sea water from the Bay tides entering the North Landing River. The present lock, dating from 1932, is 600ft x 75ft, with 16ft of depth. Sadly, for waterways enthusiasts like we are, it is the only one on the Intracoastal Waterway. We work up to pass a yacht on our port side: binoculars pick up the Red Ensign and the name, the *Regale* of London – how *did* she get here?

We came to the lock in the bright evening. Just ahead of it, a road-bridge only opens once in each hour, and we had missed it. The Corps of Engineers not having provided a set of mooring dolphins, we had to keep position under power between moored cruisers on one side and shallow water the other. The lock itself, passed at dinner-time, nearly cost Charles his dinner, but it was worth cold food.

Below, a tow was waiting to enter; beyond, the Dismal Swamp Canal branched to the left, black and gold in the sunset. Beyond again, we entered Chesapeake city on our way to moor at old Portsmouth, on our left. Across and down the river lay Norfolk, Virginia, base of the US Atlantic fleet. As we came to our mooring we passed tier after tier of older warships, then cargo ships. Ashore, we had time to walk a little way, and chose Court Street, clearly a preservation area of old wooden houses, each one delightful in its own character of verandah with rocking-chairs and pot flowers, white-pillared porch and dainty portico, well judged upper storey with shuttered windows, and sometimes little dormers. Twilight in a clear sky brought out the blue and white of bluebells and irises round pond steps. As we returned to the waterside a sliver of new moon showed, and we turned our treasured half-dollar. Lights had come on in city buildings, and were scattered through the moored boats. This was the Elizabeth River which Captain John Smith (he of Pocahontas fame) explored in 1608 and named after James I's daughter, later to be Bohemia's Winter Queen. We walked back to hear 'Daisy Bell' and 'There is a Tavern in the Town' on the saloon piano, and the beehive-like buzzing of the bridge-players.

Morning found us running up that inland sea they call Chesapeake Bay, past lighthouses, each of a different design for easy recognition, that look like houses set down on rocks or stilts. The chart showed famous names: the James River, site of Virginia's first English settlement at Jamestown and, above and to the west, the Potomac that leads to Washington and the Chesapeake & Ohio Canal. Higher still, the Susquehanna once initiated a canal line that ran past Philadelphia far inland.

The weather turned cold. We piled on jackets and jerseys in a steely late afternoon of grey sea and sky, while crabbers followed up their buoys and freighters at anchor waited for berths at Baltimore beyond the bridge at Annapolis. Small sailing-boats lean into the wind. A military plane roars overhead. 'Why?' asks a passenger. 'Target practice,' says the captain. 'On us?', with a squawk. 'Yeah. From over there – just practice.'

As we turned into Annapolis harbour and slowed, a fleet of tiny yachts with brilliant red, blue and yellow spinnakers came swiftly out past us and lit up the grey bay. A few minutes, and a gun fired. Another fleet of different yachts foamed past. We had arrived in the middle of some races.

The sun coming out as we moored in the brilliant, elegant harbour under the dignity of the Naval Academy with its echoes of Greenwich's layout, we hurried along pontoons to the street, past polished lines of all sizes of yachts perfectly moored, in water where not a piece of rubbish dared to be seen. The Annapolis Yacht Club, strictly unpretentious, spoke of quality, of (thank goodness) an elite, meaning those who believe in excellence and try to practise it.

In the evening twilight we walked up the little old town to the State House (oldest in continuous use in the United States), and enjoyed the charm of the place. A two-storeyed brick building with pillared entrance and pediment above, its six-sided dome below a lofty cupola soars high above the town and the lawns, trees and flower beds about it. It stands within State Circle. Not far away Church Circle matches it, and in between a long path of red and white azaleas leads from the gates to the correctly beautiful Governor's Mansion, for Annapolis is the capital of Maryland. Round the two Circles were narrow steep old streets, their pavements (sidewalks) brick-paved, their close-packed coloured houses gay with shutters and little porches, bow windows and steep roofs, making proper town street lines. Places of historical interest were neatly labelled, and we read 'Fleet Street 1696' with pleasure at the foot of a continuous line of uneven two-storeyed brick or timber cottages that was first cousin to many an East Anglian street.

Next morning in brilliant sunshine we took a closer look at old Annapolis. Round the mound upon which the State House stands, below the wooden fence, a May festival was being organised. We had missed yesterday's maypole and dancing; today promised art displays, flower-stalls, plants, cookery, quilting, on a long spread of stalls under bright canopies and umbrellas, while all around the dogwood and lilac and chestnut trees were out, and the gardens were bright with tulips and

Annapolis: 'we walked up to the State House . . .'

azaleas. So far on this trip we had missed town gardens comparable to London, but we had them here, in Annapolis's homely government centre. And, to add to the pleasures the locals were offered, the Annapolis Chorale were singing Beethoven's *Mass in C*, the Academy and Mary Washington College choir were doing Honegger's *King David*, and the

Dramatic Society Molière's *Misanthrope*. We would have liked to stay longer.

We moved on to pay a visit to the Naval Academy chapel. A set of blue windows was linked by the theme of water, including Christ preaching from a boat, and stilling the storm, the Ark with an elephant and his friends looking out, and Jonah going down head first into the whale. In the crypt, Paul Jones, called here the founder of the American Navy, was given very full treatment.

Our memory of Annapolis is of shining water, home-made cakes, inns and restaurants offering oysters in the shell, friendliness, spring-green chestnut and delicate pink-flowering trees, the soaring green-and-white State House dome holding the little streets together, heavy wirescape in every charming urban vista (long since invisible, we were sure, to the townspeople's eyes) and yacht masts dense as young poplar plantations.

Running up Chesapeake Bay in the afternoon sun, we look at wooded banks with low reddish cliffs, houses between the trees, and here and there a grouping that makes a village. Islands pass; yacht wings lie ahead, and the foamy wake of a cruiser comes up behind and passes; a towboat and barge meet us, then a freighter. Ahead, at the top of the bay, up the Elk River, is the 19-mile long Chesapeake & Delaware Canal, through which we shall pass to reach Delaware Bay and the New Jersey coast. It was a lock canal once; now it is a straight sea-level cut, much between high banks. We'd have liked some locks, but it *is* a real canal, and a ship canal at that.

On deck our fellow-passengers sit in the sun. Little friendly groups have formed, for we have been together nearly a fortnight. We are giving and asking addresses: we promise to write, they to call next time they are in England. It is all warm and all meant, even though, much of it, naturally evanescent. George, who subscribes to our *Waterways World* and who has powerful binoculars, briefs Charles on our position, identifies buoys, explains passing traffic, and lends charts. Leonard is a quality printer and publisher, and volunteer fireman, all very much in our experience; he is keen and knowledgeable on the history of the San José valley in California and its wine-growing industry. Mary Hazard and Alice Mary talk about poetry and women poets, and Mary gives her some splendid combined hooks and clothes pegs with which one can hang washing from a rail. John, who flirts with his wife, shows us photographs of his three pretty daughters. We find ourselves in agreement on Children and How They Should be Brought Up. The sun is warm, the water smooth. A canal lies ahead, a bottle of Mateus Rosé is in the ice-box, and this is a captain's party evening (the third so far) which means drinks on the ship and general cheerfulness.

The banks narrow, their heights patterned with the many greens of spring. Fields top hills, beach huts put hesitant toes in the water; a white house stands on top of a hill, wood-backed. We pass a marina, and steer for what seems solid hill. The canal opens up. We enter, and pass a high-level bridge, Schaefer's Canal House at Chesapeake City whose restaurant windows overlook the canal, village greens and revetted banks. Access roads parallel the water on either side and, behind them, canal cuttings curve below the fields. Then, between two piers, we are out into Delaware Bay.

Long after night has fallen we sit on deck, watching the lights of freighters inbound for Philadelphia higher up the Delaware, or for the canal and Baltimore. Charles is swapping English stories against Leonard's Californian. The crescent moon rides high above us.

Just after midnight we passed through the short Cape May Canal, and early morning found us running close to the long sand ridge of the southern New Jersey shore. This could have been a rough stretch; instead, we moved gently to the low long Atlantic rollers. No trees broke the line of a continuous sandy beach, backed by houses, bungalows and an occasional block of flats. As the ridge merged into the coastline further north, houses thickened, developments increased almost into one continuous town, and in every kind of architecture from the Victorian onward. Mile after mile it went on: maybe from the land it was exciting, homey or at any rate a change from New York, but from the sea it looked terrible.

Asbury Park gave us the first tower-block. New Yorkers and New Jersey people on board pointed out sights to Californians, who have come as far to see the Waterway as we have. Tower-blocks increased, standing high against the flatness. Long stretches of seawall protected the coast, broken here and there by lines of beach huts. A steel framework for a high-rise appears: 'That's the sort where, when you buy an apartment, they put the walls on for you', says our humorist. A hill appeared, Highlands, at the base of Sandy Hook. On it, twin lighthouse towers, between them the date 1862, one still used, the other now a museum. From the hill a long low spit of land stretched on, at the end of it the white tower of the Sandy Hook lighthouse, goal of so many seafarers.

It is 10.30am on this last full day on board. Finishing touches are being put to sketches, embroideries, knitting; library books are being skipped to see what happens. A crew member plays patience. Bob, the cook, relaxes, for the buffet lunch is prepared, and thinks of his wife whom he has not seen since the *New Shoreham* went down the Intracoastal last autumn to her winter Bahamas cruising ground. The Bahamian maids think of the southern warmth to which they will soon return, for today is chilly and misty. John maintains that it should have been warm, that American weather has changed drastically, and that it is all due to the moon shots. We murmur that English seems to be much as usual.

Up on deck, Coney Island's high-rises show up to the right; ahead, the huge twin towers of the Verrazano double-deck road-bridge linking Brooklyn on the right to Staten Island on the left, appear. We pass Swinburne, then Hoffman Island to port. Under the bridge, ships and tugs ahead, Brooklyn rises on the right. Through the mists the skyscrapers of Manhattan emerge, the soaring World Trade Center to the left. Dimly the Statue of Liberty shows green ahead. An orange-painted Staten Island ferry fusses past, and a moored oil-tanker discharges into barges alongside. Past the statue, past Ellis Island, no longer an immigration station, past Battery Park at the foot of Manhattan and the three semi-circular green arches of the ferry terminal to the East River, and a short-term mooring almost

'Through the mists the skyscrapers of Manhattan emerge . . .'

under Brooklyn Bridge. Our approach, *mutatis mutandis*, has been that of countless immigrants who over the years have come to America: hearts uplifted by Liberty; fears raised by Ellis Island; a widening future opening as they set foot on American ground. How much of feeling is missed by those who now arrive by air!

We cruise up the East River, past the United Nations building, under Queensboro Bridge with its traceried and finialed ironwork, to the left of Roosevelt Island, then to the right at Hell's Gate (so called from its tide-race) where the Harlem River runs straight ahead to join the Hudson behind Manhattan. Leftwards, New York's canyon streets open one by one as we pass by. Hell's Gate rail-bridge carries the electrified tracks of the New York, New Haven & Hartford, running into Penn station. The river widens, we pass two bridges, swing sharply to our left, and are at the beginning of Long Island Sound. To our right, Long Island, to our left the New York state and then the Connecticut shore. The East River's tides and traffic make it unsuitable for pleasure-craft, but now sailing water begins. Most islands and bays have their yacht clubs, and at summer weekends the water is white with sails.

One wishes sometimes that America would shrink. Chesapeake Bay and Long Island Sound, both so full of interest; yet, as we cruise in *New Shoreham*, their shores are hardly visible. The explorer therefore swears to himself to return, to seek smaller waters in a smaller boat, with more hours to spare and no timetable. The sea is smooth, fortunately for Alice Mary who is a bad sailor. Americans don't seem to feel queasy so quickly: maybe it's because they are brought up on rocking-chairs.

A short stop early next morning at Newport at the entrance to Narragansett Sound, a naval, shipbuilding, yachting, holiday place, and then journey's end at Warren, Rhode Island, higher up the Sound in the shipbuilding yard of Captain Luther Blount who owns the *New Shoreham* and much else, and is accounted a character. A paper is pinned to the ship's notice board: 'Happiness always. Safe journey home. The Crew.' Good-byes end many pleasant acquaintanceships. Maybe we shall meet again under English skies . . . 'Do you remember . . .?'.

'Good-bye.'

'Have a good holiday.' In a fortnight we shall be back on board, but not these others. But in California and Florida, New York and Illinois, stories will be told about the peculiar English who came to America to travel on waterways, and the strange things they said in how quaint an accent. We would like to think so.

A bus has been provided to take some of us into Providence, Rhode Island's capital. It is a yellow-painted school bus (as are all school buses in America and Canada), and in it we sweep up to the entrance of our Holiday Inn. It was, we guessed from the demeanour of the bellhop, an unexpected way to arrive. Nervously, Charles tipped him an extra dollar. Our room restored our self-confidence: it looked directly over roofs to the state Capitol building. We took the sanitised paper off the tooth-mugs, poured ourselves two gins, and looked around. Space and, American-style, two double beds. Dorothy Parker's encomium on marriage, 'the deep, deep peace of the double bed after the hurly-burly of the chaise longue' was echoed in our bodies. We had enjoyed every day of the *New Shoreham*, the nights not so much, given our six footage. Now we could stride up and down, could lie and kick and roll, could have a bath as well as a shower, were free of pressed-beef undressing and serpentine sex, and back to open plan.

Chapter 4

Water Holiday at Harpers Ferry

Before we left England we bought a fat and heavy guide to the USA to find that, except for listing hotels, it ignored Providence altogether. It was wrong: the city is full of surprises, beginning with the State House building visible from our hotel window. The Capitol at Washington has a dome, and it seems *de rigeur* for State Houses also to have domes. This has the second largest unsupported marble dome in the world – city pride in America makes splendidly big and quite uncheckable statements like that all the time – and it has given birth to quadruplets, one little 'un at each corner of its base.

A Saturday hour's walk revealed a bookshop stocking more novels with no violence and happy endings than we had seen in years; we asked a woman buying a picture-book of London whether she was about to visit it, and found her to be a 1946 GI bride from West Ham. On another street Mrs Walker tells fortunes by hand and cards. There is an Old Stone Bank, deliciously reminiscent of the Old Woollen Stocking or the Old Tow Bag. (The Bank's native caution conformed to its atmospheric name: five anxious heads met round our American Express dollar traveller's cheque before it was decided to cash it on condition that a third signature was added on the back.) Two doors down from it is an excellent cheap Italian restaurant, and round the corner the Beneficent Church (Congregational) with four huge pillars in front, a tremendous pediment, and a golden dome, faces a sex cinema advertising its current offering with an all-male cast. Grace Church (Protestant Episcopal) were doing *Noye's Fludde*, so we bought two tickets for Sunday afternoon at $3.00 each. Beyond our hotel were four more Italian restaurants and a Roman Garden. Surely there is something here for any tourist?

Next day we discovered that Benjamin Franklin's statue stands in the lobby of the Old Tow Bag. He was brought to Providence from New York in 1858 by the Propellor (propeller-driven steamboat) *Westchester*, owned by the Commercial Steamboat Company, for a freight charge of $6.50. The cheque in payment and related correspondence are framed there alongside Benjamin.

Next morning 8.34am found us on Amtrak's unwaiting-roomed Track 5, waiting in cold wind and rain for the through train to Washington, where we were to change for Harpers Ferry, a journey through eight states and the District of Columbia, most of it being a return by land along the coast we had travelled in the *New Shoreham*. She came. A huge diesel locomotive, baggage car and seven coaches, one a buffet, with the same excellent coaching stock and efficient, smartly turned-out staff as before. Railway bells are extinct in England, surviving only in pub names like that by Brighton station, but an American locomotive is 'voiced like a great bell swinging in a dome' as it arrives at and leaves a station.

The run along the coast of Rhode Island and Connecticut to New York City could be called The Water Route. Bordering Long Island Sound, one gets sight after sight of sea bays, crosses estuary after estuary tiered with moored cruisers, yachts, tugs, cranes and, now and then, sea-going ships. Famous old whaling ports like Mystic, great rivers like the Connecticut and, to our surprise, the Thames, quite as broad as its namesake, pass by, the latter with New London at its mouth, but Norwich higher up. One of the oddities of America is this juxtaposition of familiar names. In Rhode Island, Tiverton, Portsmouth and Bristol all neighbour each other, while nearby Somerset is a town and Taunton a river.

The land is watery too, swamps and small lakes a characteristic of all land we could see from the train, with the harsh gravelly soil and quarries that go with it. Other areas are richer, but though this is mid-May, beech and oak woods are still brown. Only pussy-willow cheers the swamps and blackthorn the woodland edges. No vegetable gardens round any houses yet – winter is too harsh and long. Changes in the immediate landscape were so sudden that we thought it looked as if it had not evolved but been erupted. It remains lonely, little inhabited and wild – except for the watersides where you count yachts and cruisers by hundreds, and life is busy.

Inland, swamp, marsh and fluttering swallows, heath, dogwood and straggly trees gave way to trees occasionally broken by pasture. Here was that early spring which we had left behind in England five weeks before. The day would, however, take us forward some weeks as we moved south. Houses, villages, towns, slowly closed up as we approached New York. From about Bridgeport we entered a manufacturing zone that seemed only occasionally to be broken until, hours later, we had reached Baltimore in Maryland. Across the gangway, two elderly coloured people slept in each other's arms; ahead of them, a white woman annotated a book on planning with a felt-tipped pen, and a bearded young man read a close-type paperback, *Love and Orgasm*, while eating a hamburger. A girl (she turns out to be an English nurse, three years over here) was reading T. S. Eliot.

'You enjoy him?' we asked.

'I found this paperback in a bookstore, and thought the poetry looked interesting', she replied, and read steadily for an hour or more.

Out of the window, oddities were held for a second: 'Lottie's Country Store', 'Railroad Avenue', 'Station Inn', an advertisement for Raleigh bicycles, the Devonshire Cream Mint Co, and freight cars from the Alaska and the Cadiz Railroads.

To New Haven the train has been something of a local, stopping at smallish places, but now it moves to electrified track and becomes an Inter-City. Speed has been greater than on our Chicago–Cincinnati run, the track-bed better. Mechanised track-laying is going on under the North East Corridor Improvement Program, which aims to do much what Britain did to enable high-speed trains to be run, but the equipment being used, though modern, seems less sophisticated than that to which we are used in Britain. Train equipment is good. Cafe cars provide for long journeys with neat little folding boxes to take food and drink back to your seat; toilets are well designed and make vandalism hard work, with drip soap, slot towels. We never found a wrecked one. It is probably due partly to good staff, and also to the American habit of tidiness and cleanliness.

We entered New York over the New Haven tracks we had previously seen from the East River. We saw the city, just, through thin rain and mist, and chuckled, for we had now seen New York twice, each time hidden in the sort of fog most Americans are convinced eternally covers London. Hidden skyscrapers loomed past; tenement blocks; new two-storey brick terrace housing; old and newer industrial buildings; then into tunnel and so to Penn station, dimly-lit, full of heavy pillars, a gloomier New Street, Birmingham.

Having tunnelled under the Hudson on departure, we ran fast on Penn Central tracks through an industrial belt of New Jersey and Pennsylvania. We noted a park-and-ride inter-City station at Metropark, similar in intent to Bristol Parkway, and the crossings of two rivers well known in American waterway history, the Raritan and the huge Delaware, the latter running hard with floodwater. Chestnut tree candles met us outside Philadelphia. Over the Schuylkill (another once-navigable river) and past an elephant on a weather vane at America's first zoo, and we had a sight of the fair city to the left. It is late afternoon and the sky is breaking at last.

From the *New Shoreham* we had seen the sea approaches to the ports of Philadelphia, Wilmington (Delaware) and Baltimore (Maryland), but now we ran along the edge of the land and looked outwards to see ships and the sea. Eyes caught more oddities: 'Hake Inc.'; our first gasometer; a Sunday Breakfast Mission; advertisements for Maryland Fried Chicken, and the crossing of the Susquehanna at Havre de Grace, whence the Susquehanna & Tidewater Canal once gave access to the extensive Pennsylvania Canal system. Across our gangway a plain young woman was occupying one seat, her luggage another, while her umbrella stuck out to trip the unwary. Above, the rack was empty: presumably a supporter of some lib that started and finished with herself.

We much like two features of Amtrak trains: the regular

announcement of stations a minute or two in advance of arrival, and the dealing with all tickets on trains, so doing without platform barriers and collectors. More staff travel on the trains; there are fewer on stations. Both increase the tourist's confidence in his mode of travel. The local accents of the announcers vary like our real county accents, and we keep our ears out for them.

Washington came up on time at 7.30, with no glimpse of the Capitol. Tired now, we climbed down to a platform whose canopy was supported on iron fluted columns with ramshorn capitals. Met by an old friend, and well fed in the attractive and relaxing station restaurant, we were then put on the 'Shenandoah' for the 70-minute journey to Harpers Ferry. It had become dark, and we only knew that we were climbing, and that ours was the fifth stop. At the little silent station Dixie Kilham, owner of Hilltop House hotel and descendant of an early Harpers Ferry settler, met us in his Mercedes. Five minutes of steep, narrow streets and we were at journey's end.

Next morning, weather cleared, we stood on the hotel balcony looking at a tremendous view. Left and right were lines of wooded mountains. Far below us on the left foamed the swollen muddy Potomac, under two railway-bridges, one ours of the previous evening. Beyond, just visible, the Shenandoah joined it to form the broader stream that divided the mountain ranges and disappeared into the distance. On all sides of us lay great hills, rivers and sky, in which further peaks showed in the morning mist. We were in West Virginia. Beyond the Potomac, and the derelict Chesapeake & Ohio Canal that we knew bordered it in the woods on the far side, lay Maryland. Past the Shenandoah rose the Blue Ridge mountains in Virginia; three states in sight. From below – 'hear the train blow' – came a prolonged moo that echoed up the valley, and a Baltimore and Ohio freight train slowly rumbled out of the tunnel opposite and over the Potomac bridge. 'This', we said, 'is a bit of all right', and went into breakfast.

Why Harpers Ferry? About 1933 a play called *Gallows Glorious* had been staged in London, ran for two weeks, and was taken off. It was about John Brown, and Charles, with the help

Harpers Ferry: the Potomac and, coming in on the right, the Shenandoah

of complimentary tickets from a dramatic agent friend of his, had seen it twice. Thenceforward, Harpers Ferry had been in his mind. While we were planning this tour, everything fell into place: it was on the Chesapeake & Ohio Canal, it had a hotel, there was a train service.

In 1859 John Brown, a 59-year-old anti-slavery fanatic, with an 18-man army raided the government arsenal at Harpers Ferry, hoping both to raise a negro insurrection and to gain arms to set up a free negro stronghold in the mountains. He took the place by surprise but, without either a plan to exploit success or enough men, he was driven into the armoury fire-engine house by marines commanded by Colonel Robert E. Lee. Some of his followers were killed in the fighting, some

John Brown's fire-engine house at Harpers Ferry

escaped. The rest, including Brown, were hanged. Seventeen months later the Civil War began. Since then, deservedly or not, John Brown's name, like his soul, has gone marching on. So did his fort, the engine house. Sent to the World's Columbian Exposition at Chicago in 1893 and rebuilt there, it was later reassembled beside the Shenandoah, and later again at Storer College, founded at Harpers Ferry in 1866 for the education of ex-slaves and their descendants. Itself thus only doubtfully original, it is now back on its original site.

The Harpers Ferry barber, cutting Charles's hair, did not think much of John Brown. 'Just a rebel', he said; 'It's much more important that the rifle works here made the first guns with interchangeable parts: it was a beginning of mass production.'

The barber was right. There is much more to Harpers Ferry than John Brown. It began when Robert Harper set up his ferry in 1747; it took a great step forward when George Washington encouraged Congress to buy land from the Harper family and set up a national armoury and arsenal here beside the Potomac, where water power and raw materials were available. Building began in 1796 and weapons were produced in 1801: indeed, some of them were used by Lewis and Clark, the soldiers who led the first crossing of western America from the Mississippi to the Pacific in 1804–06. So Harpers Ferry became a considerable town, with other industries also along the Shenandoah shore. However, those who had settled higher up did not want to be identified with it; therefore Bolivar was chartered as a separate town in 1797, though its main street joins that of Harpers Ferry below. Today, Bolivar is the domestic, Harpers Ferry the tourist, centre.

But the armoury was burned in the Civil War and not rebuilt. The town decayed, until it found a new life as a shopping and amusement centre for people brought by the railway. Then came the serious flood of 1924 and the disastrous hurricane of 1936; between them they ended another phase of Harpers Ferry history. Now at summer weekends the National Park Service is turning the part nearest John Brown's Fort into a replica of what it might have been in 1859, complete with Park officials and locals as replica citizens and soldiers.

As historians ourselves, we jibbed a little at such organised and simplified presentations of history, and at the underlying assumption that the little place has no present independent life to form future history. But then our tradition is different. However, the place has its own delights: the John Brown wax museum, a studio where you can be dressed in nineteenth-century costume and be tintyped, an excellent silversmith, and the sundaes of the 'Swiss Miss'. But we also liked Bolivar, which has the volunteer Friendship Fire Company, with two engines and a rescue van, a notice outside the Post Office reading 'No Loafing, Order of the Mayor', another offering 'Large Eggs, Brown', and Patches, Inc, lined floor to ceiling with quilting materials, where we bought eight quarter-yards of assorted patterns to repair our very old village-made patchwork quilt. There is also a Downing Street.

The main road runs through the beginning of Harpers Ferry on the Shenandoah water and flood level, turns a sharp angle to climb the mountains above the Potomac, and the village climbs alongside it. Wooded heights go on rising beside the road, with houses, chapels and old ruins hidden along tracks in them. The main road levels out with Bolivar into more open farming country. Spring had really come here, and we saw the delight of dogwood, pink, red or white, in its delicate graceful shape at every house and corner, irises in splendour spreading from garden into rough ground, and white violets instead of daisies in the grass between footway and road. There were even two or three patches of lettuce, spring onion, spinach. Down the steep slopes to the river the woods were in leaf, with the paulonia claimed as special to this area glowing pinkish-mauve on every sunny patch. Everybody was talking about the flood-rains and shocking weather, and said we had brought the sunshine.

But across the Potomac lay what we had come to see, the Chesapeake & Ohio Canal, result of the eastern seaboard's effort to pass the Allegheny Mountains and reach the farmlands bordering the Ohio River. Americans first tried to improve the navigation of the Potomac itself; then in 1828 they began, on the same day, to build the C&O Canal and the Baltimore & Ohio Railroad along the same strip of land on the Maryland side. The railway won the race to the Ohio, and in 1850 canal construction ended at the colliery centre of Cumberland, 185 miles from its beginning at Georgetown outside Washington. Closed after the damage caused by the 1924 flood, the C&O's 74 locks, eleven stone aqueducts and one 3,117ft tunnel lie derelict but not abandoned. They are in the care of the National Park Service, who maintain the whole length of towpath as a walking track, care for structures, maintain simple camping sites, and organise historical programmes about the canal. Restoration for navigation, to which we in England are accustomed, had been ruled out because of expense and the danger of future floods.

Our good friend Tom Hahn, then president of the American Canal Society, introduced it to us two days before he left for a month's cruise on English canals. A bright sunny day, the Potomac's falling level still showing the brown of floodwater, and stretching alongside, under arching trees of the wood's edge, the broad towpath. Beside it lay the canal's dry bed, with every now and then the stone chamber of a lock, almost the same width, but a little longer, than those on our own Grand

A lock on the old Chesapeake & Ohio Canal, the Potomac beyond

Union. The shell walls of a canalside pub, with the graffito 'John Brown Lives'; a restored lock-house; the sites of others that had been washed away; culverts; all the familiar furniture of a nineteenth-century canal.

The canal bed was cut out of the mountains along the course of the river. Sometimes the cliff rose sheer from the old water level, and one could see where rock had been blasted or levered away; sometimes it receded a little, and the waterway ran past meadow and copse. But not for long, for the cliffs returned to remind us of the engineering problems its builders had had to cope with. Cliffs, woods, canal, river, accompanied by red maples, birds and butterflies, some familiar like the swallowtail, most as unfamiliar as the bright red cardinal bird. Twice we saw a rabbit, once a poisonous copperhead snake. The canal was a sight so beautiful on this May morning that we walked in a kind of daze beside the river, below the cliffs.

Not far away was the three-arched masonry aqueduct that spans Antietam Creek, from the banks of which once came much of the iron that was used at Harpers Ferry armoury. Nearby, we had a sight of the 75ft-high stone column of the Rumsey monument. A local Shepherdstown man and one of George Washington's engineers of the Potowmack Company, predecessor of the C&O, he built a jet-propelled steamboat that successfully sailed the Potomac, doing 4mph upstream, at Shepherdstown in December 1787. Among the many candidates for the title of inventor of the steamboat, he is the local boy.

Another day we sat high above the Shenandoah on the rock where Thomas Jefferson in 1793 looked down the valley, saying afterwards that the view was 'worth a voyage across the Atlantic'. A school party approached, bunched round a stringy man of middle-age. He led them to the rock, explained it, Jefferson and the view, answered a question or two, and departed to the next item on his historical schedule. Five minutes later, a scatter of youngsters poured down the path, firing cap pistols. By the time the young, fattish man with them had caught up, they were off again, he in pursuit. No one had looked at anything. Later, in the village, we met stragglers, still firing, with no sign of him. Then, out of John Brown's Fort filed the first party, the stringy man still explaining, still answering questions.

Outside the Roman Catholic church above Harpers Ferry, a plaque relates that during the Civil War the pastor (the plaque's word) was the Rev Michael Costello, a British subject. He proceeded to hoist the British flag above the church and, seemingly, both Federals and Confederates, fearing an international incident, neither shelled nor occupied the church, 'thanks', says the plaque, 'to the Union Jack'. Presumably the ladies' sewing guild had made the flag. Midday was hot, and we indulged in life's purest pleasure in a tourist centre: sitting on a bench in the shade and watching or listening to other people, hot and earnest and clutching guide books, doing the sights.

Back at the hotel we got talking to a pleasant middle-aged couple, to find that his grandfather remembered barges on the northern section of the Wabash & Erie, his grandmother had swum in one of its aqueducts and he, once an Indiana lawyer, had often handled deeds to former canal lands. The Wabash & Erie, we feel, is becoming quite an old friend.

This is Civil War battle country. It is strange to see 'Gettysburg' on a road sign, and to meet the superintendent of Antietam battlefield at a party. Round here we sense that there is an edge, even now, to the words Federal and Confederate.

Above the little town is Harper Cemetery, entered through an archway bearing those words in cast-iron, where Robert Harper himself is buried. He died in 1782. Though only three houses had been built by then, he presciently set aside four acres of hilltop for the cemetery of the town he knew would come. Here, as in Bolivar's graveyard, the gravestones give evidence of the far places from which people had come to settle in these lonely hills – England, Germany, Ireland, the Netherlands. Home-made verses showed graves of children. One stone read 'William Broadus . . . Major in the American Army during the Revolutionary War. Died Harpers Ferry . . . 1830'. Major Broadus must have had tales to tell as an old man, in the village pub, as the rain beat down and the Potomac sounded outside: 'It was a famous victory'.

Fast-talking fast-moving Dixie Kilham of Hilltop House hotel is a character. Once a Baltimore attorney, he got himself involved in dramatic productions, and bought a decayed hotel on the highest point here above the Potomac (where in the past Mark Twain, Alexander Graham Bell [to get away from the telephone] and President Woodrow Wilson had stayed) as a place for putting on drama. From a wall of old cuttings we at once spotted Basil Rathbone.

Having got it, he slowly turned it into the idiosyncratic hotel it is now, a place where families and honeymoon couples come and loud-voiced drinking types are told there is no room. It is also, however, a sizeable conference centre and a mecca for tourist bus lunches. We once collected small states, and spent time in Liechtenstein and San Marino. There we had something of the same feeling as at Hilltop House – quiet nights and domestic mornings; the appearance of shoals of tourists;

souvenir-buying, eating, all the business of 'Isn't that cute?' and 'Let's take this for Auntie Maud'; then the revving up and the climbing in, and back everything sinks to local feeling once again. We chuckled as Sunday came, with crowds of children at their maximum. A notice 'Out of Order' at once appeared on the colour television set in the lounge. It had been in order on Saturday for the Preakness Stakes horserace at Baltimore which the locals all wanted to see, and would, we reckoned, be in order again in the evening. It was. In a hidden world of separation, conferences went on, unnoticed by residents and lunchers alike.

Dixie Kilham took to us, maybe because he recognised two fellow eccentrics. We certainly took to him. By our second evening he had produced his written family history (his family comes from Kilham near the Driffield Navigation in Yorkshire, which Charles knew), showed us round the hotel at cantering speed, introduced us to his mother, a brisk lady of 80-odd, and insisted on moving us to his lushest room at no extra charge. Two days later, he and Anita asked us to a private dinner, the first time in our lives a hotelier had done so. Half a dozen friends were there, so that we had a valuable mix with locals on a normal, non-travelling level. We ate and drank well above our station, Dixie completely at leisure and unprofessional. We felt the invitation and evening were remarkable tributes to an American hotel owner.

Oddly, no footbridge connects Harpers Ferry to the Chesapeake & Ohio's towpath on the Potomac's far bank, and it's a long way round by road, as Tom Hahn had taken us. However, a kindly official at the railway station (railwaymen have a kinship with canal enthusiasts) gave us permission to walk along the footway of the less-used railway bridge. Across, we could stroll at will on the towpath in the chequered sunshine. As the river level dropped, white water showed around the rocks, its colour changed from brown almost to green, little stony beaches appeared below the canal's riverside walling, though a fringe of trees still stood in floodwater. Huge yellow and dark purple butterflies fluttered across the path; a squirrel ran in front of us before scuttling up a tree to lie flat on a branch and peer at us passing below; mallard rose from a watered stretch of canal, and two elderly fishermen came up from the river bank, rod in hand, string of fish in the other. High on its wooded hill over the water our hotel smiled at us.

To visit a lower section of canal we went with Ellwood Wineholt, a National Park Service ranger, to take a school party down to the towpath for a combined canal/natural history morning. In a school bus, riding with thirty-six assorted 11-year-olds from outlying Washington, we wound along country lanes to the canal. Everyone talked at once at the tops of their voices. Now and then they broke into song: a hymn (it was a church-run school) or a numbers song about 'seven little Indian girls' which went with rhythmic handclapping, punctuated by shouts of 'Excuse me' from the teacher in charge when she wanted silence for a bit of instruction. She got it, too, though the margin was narrow.

Arrived on the towpath, Ellwood talked to the children while we explored. Every now and then a phrase floated back from the teacher: 'Point of Rocks to Harpers Ferry – write it down, children' or 'You haven't asked the rats, gnats, snakes if you can come here where they live, so you must respect them; how would you like them walking uninvited through your room?' from Ellwood. He could answer all our queries of names of trees and plants. We walked along the towpath to the ruined Catoctin Creek aqueduct, once a three-archer, now with one arch remaining, the rest washed out in a 1973 flood. Stone-built, with great masonry wingwalls and abutments, it stands defiant yet beside the two-arched railway viaduct alongside.

Later that day we saw Monocacy, built of white granite, the biggest on the canal, comparable to our own Lune aqueduct on the Lancaster Canal. Monocacy, 516ft long, with seven 54ft arches, finished in 1833, is enormously impressive, its grandeur marred only by the lacing of external and internal steel struts that support it after Hurricane Agnes's damage in 1972. Hopefully, the Park Service wait for the money to reinstate it.

Then back to Harpers Ferry on the school bus: scream, scream, but no eating, no litter. 'Excuse me, children – this is the Potomac River' . . . 'Excuse me, excuse me, this is the

Shenandoah River'. We de-bus to a chorus of good-byes, a forest of hands. Behind us we left notebooks filled with indecipherable graffiti that would, the indomitable elderly teacher assured us, be sorted out at a recapitulation class that evening. We staggered home.

Our last day fulfilled a dream, to see the Portage Railroad, perhaps the most romantic transport line ever built anywhere. In Pennsylvania, some hundred miles north of Harpers Ferry, we had tried to plan it into our trip, and had failed. It seemed unreachable in the time we had available, until Lee Struble of the Park Service offered to drive us there. Blessings, Lee, upon your head: we had accepted before she had finished the sentence.

In 1826, alarmed by the trade advantage given to New York by the opening the previous year of the Erie Canal from the Hudson River to Lake Erie, and its instantaneous success as a trade and passenger route to the West, Philadelphians decided upon a reply. That year the Pennsylvania legislature authorised the Main Line. It finished by being railway from Philadelphia to Columbia, canal thence to Hollidaysburg, portage railroad over Allegheny Mountain to Johnstown, canal once more to Pittsburgh on the Ohio River, in all 118 miles of railroad and 276 of canal, the whole opened in 1834.

The 37 miles of the Portage Railroad itself consisted of ten double-tracked, steam-engine-operated inclined planes, linked by sections of more or less level track worked first by horses, later by locomotives. Five planes took freight and passenger cars from Hollidaysburg to the summit, where Samuel Lemon built a house to refresh the weary traveller; five more planes returned the line to the canal level at Johnstown. The line included 300yd Staple Bend tunnel, the first in the United States for a railway. Early on, inventive types realised that if boats were built in two or three sections that could be coupled up for canal travel and separated to be put on trucks, they could pass through the whole line. Soon the odd sight could be seen of canal boat families riding out of Philadelphia in their boats, and later being hauled up the planes – what a story for children then to tell in their old age!

Sylvester Welch, the Portage Railroad's engineer, and Samuel Jones, superintendent, built it in three years from the authorising Act of 21 March, 1831. Welch was appointed on the 30th, and on 18th March 1834 he had the whole line open for use, an almost incredible feat of organisation, given the terrain and the difficulties of working in the winter.

To get canal boats on to trucks, they had to be hauled up inclines by hempen ropes which often gave way. The problem enabled an immigrant from Germany, John A. Roebling, to try out his idea for a wire rope. He bought wire and made one, 600ft long and about one inch in diameter, on his farm, and fitted it at a Johnstown boat incline. It suited, and within a few years the hempen ropes of the inclines themselves had been replaced by wire rope up to 6,400ft long. Roebling was to go on to use his wire rope in suspension bridges: we had seen one of them at Cincinnati.

The Main Line was short-lived, for in 1854 the continuous rail line over the mountain opened by the Pennsylvania Railroad replaced it. But in its day, the Portage Railroad was a wonder, and we went to see it, we two, Lee, and a college student interested in Park work called Tom.

On a lovely day we ran upstream beside the Potomac along Maryland's northern border, then turned north through shallow Pennsylvanian valleys with coloured wooden houses under trees, and the first blossom of pears, apples and plums. The hills begin; houses become fewer, and we get a glimpse of deer. Country-smoked ham is advertised, and a wayside sign says: 'Ice Cold Cider. As Much as You can Drink, 25c' (about 15p then). Sadly, it meant apple juice. We turn west on to the Pennsylvania Turnpike, a great toll-road that runs through cuttings and tunnels, over bridges and embankments, to do now much of what the old Main Line did a century and a quarter ago. We pass superbly farmed country, with the big farmhouses of Dutch settlers, small new churches, industry in some valleys – 'Wurlitzer, Pianos'. Then we turn north again, and there to our left rises the long height of Allegheny Mountain.

Clutching our Park Service guide and map, we find the foot of the long grassy slope that was once Incline 8, the middle one of the eastern five, 3,117ft long with 308ft vertical lift. On again, to the foot of Incline 6, 2,714ft long and with a vertical rise of 266½ft, the topmost of the eastern series. The foot of the slope ran under a preserved skew bridge that once carried a toll-road, beside which is a Portage Railroad memorial with useful pictures and text in cast metal. And so up beside the grassy slope to Lemon House at the top, 2,291ft above sea level, and 1,380ft above Hollidaysburg where the eastern canal ended and, we would think, the highest point to which a canal-boat has ever risen in the world.

Lemon House is now a Park Service centre, with a nice little museum, literature on sale, and a viewing room where in a few minutes a slide show gives the visitor an outline of the Main Line's story. Outside, the foundations of the engine house have been excavated and a section of incline track relaid with replica iron strips on wooden rails. Further back, digging has revealed the four lines of stone blocks that carried the iron chairs and wedged iron edge-rails (they came from south Wales) of the double-track lines connecting the two summit planes. On their knees on the muddy ground, two serious young girl archaeologists are scraping mud from some wooden sleepers, perhaps from later patching of the track. Past them ran the old line, a grassy dandelion-gold path between the trees. We followed its direction a short distance to the mountain's summit, until there lay, distant, grey, misty before us, the Ohio valley, the West, the promised land, the area that those who promoted and built so many early canals and railroads – Erie, Pennsylvania Main Line, Chesapeake & Ohio Canal, Baltimore & Ohio Railroad, James River & Kanawha Canal – had all sought to reach. What a sight it must have been to those who travelled the Portage Railroad!

Charles Dickens did so in 1842, and wrote: 'Occasionally the rails are laid upon the extreme verge of a giddy precipice; and looking from the carriage window, the traveller gazes sheer down, without a stone or scrap of fence between, into the mountain depths below.' We envied him indeed, though he was more insouciant about the inclined planes that we might have

Replica rails on Incline 6 of the Portage Railroad, 2,291ft up on Allegheny Mountain

been: 'The journey is very carefully made, however; only two carriages travelling together; and while proper precautions are taken, is not to be dreaded for its dangers.' Another traveller, who wrote as Peregrine Prolix, was jumpier: 'The ascending apprehension has left you, but it is succeeded by the fear of the steep descent which lies before you; and as the car rolls along on this giddy height, the thought trembles in your mind, that it may slip over the head of the first descending plane, rush down the frightful steep, and be dashed into a thousand pieces at its foot.'

We took the homeward road tired but exhilarated, for we had done it; we had seen the Portage Railroad. As we came into Harpers Ferry in the evening, the locust (acacia) trees were all in bloom, their scent heavy in the air.

At 7am the next morning Dixie Kilham drove us to the

station, and helped us and our luggage up past the commuters into the high coach. Below the track lay the stone boundary wall of the Armoury; in front the Potomac and the C&O Canal; to the right the village and the Shenandoah. High behind us, the sun caught the windows of Hilltop House. We waved, and were gone.

Approaching New York on our way back to Providence, we got talking to a young man with a rucksack, off to England with Freddie Laker: 'Whatever did you find to do for ten days at Harpers Ferry?' he asked us.

Chapter 5

By Hudson and Erie to the Seaway

We re-entered our Providence hotel for a little relaxation before joining *New Shoreham* again for her voyage north to Canada. But we hadn't realised either that it was graduation day at the university, or Memorial Day weekend. The hotel was full of Rhode Island veterans in embroidered forage caps, and when we observed one of them pushing into the lift a four-wheeled luggage trolley piled head-high with quarts of Scotch and cases of beer, we realised that the celebrations would be formidable. Moreover, the dining-room was full of family groups: just-graduated young men and women surrounded by celebrating grandparents, parents, brothers, sisters, uncles and aunts.

The following early morning hours were punctuated by the crashes of veterans trying to find their rooms, or their friends' rooms in order to tell them the story they had only just remembered, or the lift gates, or the ice machine. Voices were raised in protestations of eternal friendship, drowned every now and then by the howls of babies awakened by graduates anxious to share their joy with the younger generation. Every now and then our bedroom wall shook as our neighbours stumbled over the furniture, fell out of bed, or turned on the shower when they meant to flush the toilet. Having made sure we knew where the fire escapes were, we took it philosophically. But it was not relaxing.

The next day the sun was shining as we wove through departing veterans, their forage caps now drooping a little, and the crates of empties, to our taxi. But there at Warren was the *New Shoreham*, and our old friends – Captain Bob, first mate Jim, Céline the purser, and Virginia Cheetham our pen-friend of English days when we had been arranging the trip. But the cook was new. Bob was having time with his family. We glowed with ill-disguised proprietorship, for we knew the ship, we had been here before, we were the old hands. We looked pityingly at newcomers wondering which way to turn at the top of the gangway. We knew, and were content.

4pm. One and three on the hooter. Back out, swing and forward between the markers, our course set down Narragansett Bay, past the bell-buoy, among the cruisers and the flocks of white-sailed yachts, in the clouded sunshine. We were off. The waves sparkled, the passengers got acquainted. Dinner was served early as we began to roll upon rounding Point Judith into Block Island Sound on our way to New York. And then the fog came down.

Our deck-cabin proved to be a few feet from the foghorn, and immediately under the step down from the wheelhouse, so that every time the captain handed over to the mate and shot out for one reason or another, his jump landed him a few inches from Charles's right ear, lying in his upper bunk. As the foghorn sounded, and the radar brought the ship to slow or stop again and again as fog-bound anchored yachts were picked up on the screen, Charles began to wonder whether he should collect life-jackets from the lounge lockers, Alice Mary whether she should dress before putting them on.

Yet when morning came we were in the East River approaching misty New York, only an hour or two behind schedule. The fog, thinning now, followed us as we rounded Battery Park and began our voyage up the Hudson River, Manhattan to our right, the Jersey shore to the left. Skyscrapers gave way to high-rises, they to houses and industry. Then on the left the hills began, to become the cliffs of the Palisades; the river widened, and we passed Sing Sing prison – shades of Edward G. Robinson films. The hills rose higher, on both sides now, and the channel closed in upon the river's turnings.

The fog clears, yachts, cruisers, speedboats and water-skiiers come out to play. Tugs take empty oil-barges downstream, Sugarloaf Hill shows ahead, hills unfold behind hills, introductions to the Adirondack Mountains. A hundred and forty years ago the Hudson would have been alive with

'West Point Military Academy shows ahead to port, pile upon pile rising from the water's edge'

steamboats serving the towns and villages along the river, and with tugs hauling barges to and from the Erie Canal to Buffalo and the West. Today we, bound for the Erie's successor, the New York State Barge Canal, represent them all, as our white forefoot cuts a line between the frisking speedboats. Yet not quite all, for later in the day a big three-decker of the Day Line passed us, well filled with holidaymakers.

The high walls of the Adirondacks control the scenery, wooded and breaking out into massive features of rock. The sky is different, clouds vaporous not cotton-woolly. They blend and disappear into the distance like some romantic painting. A waterfall slips down the mountain; half-hidden in the woods, rising like Rhine castles from the rock, straddling a ridge, the great mansions begin to appear. Famous West Point Military Academy shows ahead to port, pile upon pile of pink-red rising like a walled city from the water's edge. Below it, an enormous triple-headed freight train rumbles past.

Tidal to Troy whither we are bound, above New York State's capital at Albany, the Hudson is named after Henry Hudson the Elizabethan explorer, who sailed the river in 1609, hoping it would lead him to the North West Passage. It didn't, but what a sight for Hudson's sailors it must have been. They are quoted as saying: 'A verrie good land to fall with and a pleasant land to see.' Hudson's river is leading us, not to the North West Passage, but to the Barge Canal and the St Lawrence, and yet . . . haven't we seen something like this before, in the Rhine gorge or approaching the Iron Gates of the Danube?

The sun begins to set behind the Catskill Mountains and their memories of boyhood enthralment with the tale of Rip van Winkle. Round the piano after dinner a little group have been singing 'In the Shade of the Old Apple Tree', 'Daisy Bell' and 'I've Been Working on the Railroad'. On deck, others watch the river unfolding in a perfect evening. The tide is with us, we are running at full speed, and shall soon pass the lights of Albany and the ocean-going ships moored in its port, to be raised through Troy lock on the Hudson River, maintained, unlike those on the Barge Canal, by the Corps of Engineers. Thus we shall be ready for the Waterford flight in the morning. At Troy the wheelhouse will be lowered (it takes to pieces, and our cabin is right underneath) in order to clear the canal-bridges with six inches to spare. We have arranged to be called at 5am, ready for the start. Sleepless perhaps, in Charles's case unshaven, we shall be on deck, for the Waterford flight, raising the waterway over 185ft through five locks, is a SIGHT. So, indeed, is the Barge Canal, second successor of the original Erie, most famous of all American canals.

Only a few inland canals around the world have really caught the imagination of men: the Erie is one. It had no American precedents. When the New York State legislature authorised it in 1817, the United States' longest canal was the 27¼-mile Middlesex, upwards from Boston. The state's population was not much more than a million, the country largely unsettled through which it proposed to build a 363-mile-long barge canal from Troy on the Hudson by way of the Mohawk River valley to Buffalo on Lake Erie. But it had great advantages; no intervening mountain range, but instead a gradual rise from the Hudson for 650ft to near Buffalo, and ample water. Begun in 1817, 40ft wide, 4ft deep, with 83 locks each 90ft x 15ft, it was built by New York State itself. With De Witt Clinton as the driving force, and men like Benjamin Wright in charge who learned their engineering on site, the whole line was opened in October 1825. It was at once a wild, unparalleled, extraordinary success, which opened up the North-East to industry and commerce, facilitated travel and emigration to the West, enormously reduced freight rates, greatly increased property values, and set off a canal boom throughout the whole United States.

The Erie gave birth to a whole range of balladry and song. Perhaps the best known song begins:

We were forty miles from Albany,
Forget it I never shall;
What a terrible storm we had that night,
On the E-ri-e Canal.

with the refrain:

Oh the E-ri-e was a-rising,
And the gin was getting low,
And I scarcely think we'll get a drink
'Till we get to Buffalo,
'Till we get to Buffalo.

But we ourselves much like this tender ballad:

John Mueller was a mule driver
On Erie's verdant shore,
His walk was humble, but his gait
Was something to adore.

The lockman's lovely daughter
Had for him a passion strong;
Although she was both short and small,
She vowed she'd love him long.

Her father's haughty castle
Stood beside the proud Mohawk;
He did not lock her in the keep,
But kept her in the lock.
(Lionel D. Wyld, *Low Bridge! Folklore and the Erie Canal*)

Enlargement was authorised as early as 1837: more followed, and trade leaped up again as sections of what amounted to a new canal were opened, the last in 1862. Finally, in 1903, New York State decided to build an entirely new and much larger waterway to take barges carrying up to 2,500 tons, which would make as much use as possible of existing lakes and rivers. This was the New York State Barge Canal; it was opened throughout in 1918. Our section, from the Hudson River to Oswego on Lake Ontario, has a depth of 13ft over lock-sills, and locks 328ft long by 45ft wide.

On deck in the dawn air at 5.30, we found that a large oil-barge and following tug lay behind us, then sadly watched them pass as the lock-lights turned green. A pause followed. We watched the reflections of every bird, leaf and cloud in the still water; listened to fish jumping, water rustling. The lock-tender was perhaps finishing his breakfast, or perhaps had urgent work in his garden. Not till Jim Lodge had been despatched on an expedition of reconnaissance and expostulation did the lock empty again, and we move in. It was nearly 7.00.

The five locks are close together. Mitre-gated, concrete-walled, they were wonders to those of the passengers who had never seen a lock before. Two hours later, moving forward from the wide view of fields and hills that rose behind, we passed out of lock 6, down a rocky cutting, past two vertically-rising flood-gates into the dammed-back Mohawk River, lying calm and islanded in the sunshine. Every now and then a glimpse opens of the old Erie, which runs for long distances close by the river on its southern side, with aqueducts bridging little Mohawk tributaries. On the approaches to lock 7 we could pick out first an aqueduct, then the line of the old canal half-hidden in the trees. Above locks 12 and 15 we shall catch sight of them again. In the distance is the barge and towboat that had supplanted

Climbing the Waterford locks of the New York State Barge Canal

us. We slip past them on the Schenectedy stretch to lock 8.

The broad line of the Hudson behind us, we have taken to smaller channels; 14 rising locks are ahead, using the Mohawk River, a canal stretch, and then the Oneida River. At lock 10 there were cries for Charles, and on the lockside stood George and Carol Ryon from the Atlantic Intracoastal trip, come to greet us and watch the boat go through. Amsterdam slips past, its factory buildings sizzling in the summer sun, while we sit cool beneath the deck awning. When the shade temperature is 93°, can there be any better way to travel than this, on the *New Shoreham*, with this pleasant company of waterway pilgrims, through meadows, woods and towns, past inlets, bridges and local history backed by the distant Adirondacks, pottering along at ten knots, the scenery brought to us as we sit in our deckchairs, sipping iced lemonade?

We have now become adjusted to a different temporal scale of history, to a country where a hundred years is old, two hundred very old. Our canal guide tells us of the 1773 building on the lockside at Amsterdam and, being so adjusted, we took its picture. It was erected here beside the Mohawk fifty years before the first Erie Canal was built, and so is historical indeed. The day goes gently on. We notice the scarcity of swallows, and of vegetable gardens.

We pass Fultonville, and the premises of the White Mop Wringer Co – we must get one of those. A canoe passes, paddled Indian fashion, for this is *The Last of the Mohicans* country. Just above lock 16 we pass a long low red building, the Barge Inn, evocative of an English canalside pub, and enter a mile or so of true canal section by-passing a river bend, the first so far. As evening comes on, the air cools. Strollers at a lockside carry tired children and smile at us. The green country and shining water seem asleep as we pass quietly through. Ahead, the glowing sun lights a pinkish glow upon the channel, as fishermen climb up the bank to avoid our wash breaking on the stone revetments of the channel's edge. Away on the right the Mohawk curves and twists, waiting for us to rejoin it. Before the junction, vertically-raised flood-gates reflected in the water produce a *trompe d'oeil* of solidity that puzzled even Jim the helmsman, who had to use binoculars to reassure himself of passage beneath. 'It's just like Alice going through the looking glass', said the little man with the film camera.

The lights were on at Little Falls lock as we approached. The deepest on the canal at 40½ft rise, it is also the only one to have a vertically-rising bottom gate, like the flood-gates we had just passed, instead of the usual mitres. It was dripping as we went in from just having been raised, and squealing passengers on the foredeck ran for shelter. But they were enthralled all the same, as we slowly came up in the vast dark chamber until we could see a star dead ahead, that led us to our mooring.

Wednesday, 5.15am, and we are moving quietly along the canal stretch beyond lock 18 as we come out on deck. Early morning lorries, lights still on, cross the bridges over our path. A party of boys, clustered round two camping vans, wave frantically, but there are only half a dozen of us to answer. A light mist lies over the canal; the river lies below to our right, and we look down through trees for glimpses of it. Navigation lights still blink in the coming day as flood-gates, huge in verticality, come up beside lit buildings, presaging a return to the river. To starboard a suction dredger lies huddled, its crew still sleeping. To north and south the mountains lie grey, waiting for the sun; ahead, a bell sounds faintly, perhaps in thanksgiving for such an early world.

There is coffee in the saloon – there always is – and with it we nibble biscuits and eat chocolate. The marina at Ilion (no topless towers here) offers ice, diesel fuel and showers, in that order. Pink begins to touch the north-eastern hilltops to our right, as we gently break the mirrored water. Captain Bob, in striped jersey, holds the wheel in one hand and drinks coffee with the other. When it is warmer, he will tell dry local stories in a Maine accent. Round these parts, the early settlers must have stiffened themselves with thoughts of classical civilisation in their efforts to conquer the wilderness. It shows in their place-names: Troy, Ilion, Utica, Rome.

It is 6am, river now exchanged for canal; and the sun is up, bright in a clear sky. It is going to be another hot day. We could do this for a pastime, as Westcountry people say – do this for a career is, we are told, the American equivalent. But the potential settlers in the West who crowded the packet-boats of the original Erie Canal must have woken each morning with both excitement and apprehension, as the ribbon of canal ahead called them towards hope, but away from familiarity. Lock 19. It is odd that neither approach walls nor mooring dolphins are provided for waiting craft. The boat has to be held in the lock-cut, while we hope no barge will emerge as the gates open. A lock dog stands at the stairway top, superintending our approach. No one talks much, we just look, and breathe.

We pass the branch canal and lock to Utica to our left, and come to a new experience, a section of straight canal marked as 'Seaplane landing area'. As in Norway, we notice that in these watered areas seaplanes are used as taxis. We'd like to see one. In an hour we pass one house. Lock 20 takes us to the 18-mile-long summit level, 420ft above Troy, its banks thick with the pink and white of wild honeysuckle. The grass is still wet with dew, and birds are running in it, taken by surprise at our arising from the lock.

The long summit unrolls to lock 21, the first downwards, and a wonder to some passengers. Charles has spent some time explaining to enquirers what a lock does: one hazarded the idea that its purpose was to overcome the curvature of the earth. Lock 22, a straight stretch, a curve to the left, past a suction-dredger on one side and a holiday camp on the other, past Greg's Seafood Home (Lobsters and Clams), an old-fashioned roundabout and the Canal View Cafe, and sandy-beached Lake Oneida lies before us, our track buoyed for some 21 miles to the other side at Brewerton. Lunch was a buffet on deck – tuna salad, cole slaw, crisps and gherkins, butterscotch cookies and fruit salad.

So into the Oneida River as the heat came on. How green this country is in early summer! At Brewerton lawns surround holiday bungalows, and run down to the water. Between, long stretches of woodland are still light with early greenery. Later, maybe, the grass will brown, the trees darken. But now the long green avenue to lock 23 is delightful to the eye. This has good moorings on approach walls: it is neat with white-painted fencing, and bollards and machinery boxes in the canal colours of blue and yellow. A pale-green-painted flood-gate protects the lock, there are white-painted and green-roofed lock- and control-houses, while to the left under the trees is a canal park well set out with wooden tables and chairs, each table with its own covered trash can, all ready for gongoozlers (an English canal term for those who sit or stand to look at boats). Beyond, we are a white boat in a green world, out of which lead creeks, tributaries, streams, and in which are cottages, landing stages or nothing at all but green. A candled chestnut brings back memories of matches on village cricket grounds that fade with the tree's loss.

And so we reach Three River Point (the rivers are the Oneida, Oswego and Seneca) where, unsignposted, we swing away from the main line of the Barge Canal and turn to the north down the canalised Oswego River to Oswego on the southern shore of Lake Ontario.

Down the branch waterway is Phoenix. Phoenix has character; Phoenix has things the way it likes them. It has a nice old-fashioned arched bridge across the river and a lift-bridge leading into the lock-cut. The lock itself forms part of the town square and is just the thing to amuse the children. Not content with one road across the cut, however, Phoenixians have put a drawbridge across the lock-chamber itself, and a third bridge below the lock-tail, so that they can cross just where they like, and no nonsense. Or perhaps they mark old Indian trails, and no one is going to interfere with them. We took to Phoenix. A grey heron flew along the bank by us as we left the town.

The Oswego branch drops steeply through 119ft in 24 miles and seven locks, past Fulton with its hydro-electric station and pleasant looking Lock Restaurant, to Oswego where the river runs into Lake Ontario. Here we are at the frontier: Canada is across the water.

In this spot, slightly dreary in the late afternoon, we went liquor-hunting, that curious American occupation that has no English or European equivalent. It is rather like the treasure hunts of our youth. Enquiries yield clues: two blocks this way, three blocks that, past the Laundromat, beyond Joe's Pub. When we arrived, we found a highly respectable off-licence, in this case kept by a pretty young woman with a baby and toddler to help her.

Clutching our Gordon's gin and Mateus Rosé, we returned via a two-storeyed fire-station of Edwardian period, built in liver-coloured brick, and pleasant leafy streets. No less than three churches (one offering on the same noticeboard for Saturdays a Vigil Mass at 5.15 and Bingo at 7.45) and a synagogue surrounded a square where horse chestnuts were in bloom. There too was a Civil War memorial. The stark statement that of 837 men who enlisted from Oswego county, only 147 returned, brought home the ferocity of that internecine struggle; it reminded us a little of those terrible German Second World War memorials we had seen, carrying long lists of those 'missing in Russia'. Near it, children were playing baseball. We came back to *New Shoreham* past an embattled, turreted, old-fashioned, determinedly-learned public library built in 1855, and the flashing lights of '50 Varieties of Donuts'. Now that the low bridges of the Barge Canal are past, our wheelhouse and radar have been raised again, and we are for the deep.

We sailed at 5am, out into Lake Ontario, to run almost north across its eastern end to the beginnings of the Thousand Islands archipelago (in fact, there are a lot more than that), part in Canada and part in the United States, that marks the entrance to the St Lawrence. A few rough moments, and *New Shoreham* settled down to a smooth trip of 60-odd miles to Alexandria Bay, last stop for the ship on American soil.

Jacques Cartier in 1535 named the great river that flows out of Lake Ontario the St Lawrence, whose day it was when he discovered it. But from the 1780s, men have worked to make it a better ship channel to the Great Lakes, building bigger and bigger locks, wider and deeper channels, until now the St Lawrence Seaway, opened in 1959, has created a new geography in the valley down to Montreal: new islands, new lakes, towns and villages on new sites.

By 9.30 we were among the islands. They were mostly long and thin, nicely fitted with trees, cottages, houses with towers or lookouts, boatyards, stages, barns and farmland, waterside villages; even little hills, according to taste. We are in fir country now; they darken every clump of trees. There's nothing like boat travel for making one hungry: we've eaten a large breakfast, and are already ready for lunch.

We delight in our fellow passengers. They take much trouble to bring us things they think might interest us. One has just given us an Amish-Mennonite newspaper; we find that we went past the edge of this sect's country on our drive through Pennsylvania to the Portage Railroad. Others bring us leaflets they have found, postcards, books that might bear upon our interest in waterways, or watch out for something English, that they can press on us. They praise such English institutions as they know, ask our advice about visits, tell us of their origins. It may not go very deep, but it is perfectly sincere, and we appreciate it.

The islands close in; a ferry-boat passes in one direction, a Lakes-bound Greek freighter, the *Peter L*, in the other. Wellesley Island shows ahead, and the high suspension bridge that marks the channel to Alexandria Bay. A Canadian laker (a craft specially built to fit the Seaway locks) passes us, also Lakes-bound.

Alexandria Bay is a village that exists for boat or island people: a comfortable little place of marinas, waterside motels, eating places, re-stocking places and souvenir shops. Boat trips round the islands compete with Cavallario's Steak and Sea Food House, Wally's Pizza, Ye Old Cream Shoppe, bait and fishing guides, WORMS (the word solitary across a window), and shrimp dinners at $3.35. All is enclosed within clumps of lilac bushes and lines of shady trees. There we used up on postcards the last of our American stamps. Britain might well copy two services provided by many post offices, a xeroxing machine and the sale of bags for posting books and papers. Once we had discovered the second, the problem of getting our collection of leaflets, booklets, charts and sugar wrappings home was solved: we bought bags as we went along, and posted them to ourselves.

In the late afternoon, motoring along the placid river between green banks scattered with houses and occasionally punctuated with little towns, we came to Canadian Prescott opposite United States Ogdensburg. Locking away our American dollar bills, we took out our Canadian, with their familiar pictures of the Queen. It felt comfortable to return to a monarchical system. Prescott was remarkable only in being Canadian. French appeared on notices, the main street was the 'King's Highway', 'Ltd' replaced 'Inc', and branch banks appeared. Two things interested us as we strolled, a red squirrel climbing up one side of a house to disappear with a whisk of its tail over the ridge, and a notice: 'Open House. 7 June 1978, 2–4pm, to celebrate Mrs Jane Bennett's 100th birthday'. She had six days to go and we wished her well, wondering whether the Queen sends congratulatory telegrams in Canada as she does in Britain.

5am found Charles on deck as *New Shoreham* backed out of the

Coastguard wharf and set off down the St Lawrence Seaway, straight into the red eastern clouds that lay ahead. A mile in front, a lit ship is going our way; doubtless we shall meet at Iroquois lock, five miles away, first of the seven that will take us down to Montreal. The river's current runs quite fast past the straining buoys. Lines of light on either bank slowly fade with the coming day. Behind, Prescott light double-flashes beyond the international bridge. A grain terminal and a smell of malting comes up and passes: it probably dates from pre-Seaway days, when big ships from the Lakes brought grain here for transhipment to smaller ships able to pass the then St Lawrence locks.

We catch up the freighter and fall in line behind. She is the *Kathleen* of Monrovia, Liberia, but underneath, *Fortuna*, London, shows faintly. A morning shower drives us brave half-dozen to the bridge's shelter. Our freighter moves to port and we follow. Ahead, long lines of greenish lights show us the lock, one with a fall of only a few feet that replaces the former Galop Canal that once by-passed river rapids here. The entrance light shows green for us. A line of poplars, clearly a windbreak for entering ships, backs the lock approach to our left, an artificial island to our right.

Here Charles sees his first sector-gates, used where extra strength is demanded. They are mitres, but shaped like slices of cake pivoted on their edges. On each side of the lock-gates, ship-arresters drop – arms and cables that can stop a ship threatening to hit the gates. To starboard stretches an enormous river weir. It is all totally different from the little Mohawk River and the State Barge Canal edged with farmland.

Out into the broad islanded river as we take the American side towards the Seaway's two United States locks, Eisenhower and Snell built to by-pass the old Cornwall Canal on the Canadian side that took the previous ship channel round the Long Sault rapids. *Sir Denys Lowson*, Algoma Central Marine, comes upstream and passes us, probably carrying iron ore from eastern Quebec. Ahead is red-hulled *Kathleen*; if we stick to her, we should have a comfortable transit through the locks.

In Iroquois lock of the Seaway with Kathleen

Iroquois appears on the Canadian side, a new town built before Seaway construction flooded the old one. We all answer the call to breakfast – never have we eaten grapefruit as juicy and delicious as we find here. The best don't cross the Atlantic.

We entered the Wiley–Dondero approach canal, and at 8.30, the sun breaking through and catching the *Kathleen* in brightness ahead, we came to Eisenhower past three families of wild geese visiting the lock approach. Mitre-gates this time, a 30ft drop, and we follow *Kathleen* out, a duckling behind its mother. Her crew take our photographs; we reciprocate. The lock-master hands down a box of leaflets about the Seaway for Jim to distribute. The captain sounds the hooter and it sticks, rises three notes and trembles, with bass toots. Joy among the passengers as Bob thumps it! Laker after laker, all Canadian, pass going upstream. Seven pylons on each side carry power lines across the channel, presumably originating at the hydro-electric stations beside these locks. An eighth is being built, and we are told the men working on it are probably Red Indians, who specialise in such work.

Above Snell, deepest of the Seaway locks at 47ft, *Kathleen* and we wait in the sunshine and calm, then move forward. Ahead, a huge upcoming freighter is starting to leave the lock in a quick cloud of diesel exhaust. With her are a tug and a pleasure-cruiser. Up in the wheelhouse, traffic control talks to the captain by radio telephone. We sink in the lock until our masthead is below ground level, and only *Kathleen's* deckhouse and exhaust funnel is above it. Smoothly we move out into Lake St Francis, 27 miles of river made into lake by the elimination of the Soulanges rapids. Now we enter Canada, for here the international boundary leaves the river.

We spend the middle of the day crossing the long lake to enter the Seaway's new Beauharnois approach channel on the southern side that leads to the two 42ft Beauharnois locks. The former Soulanges Canal, like that at Cornwall, by-passed the river's rapids to the north. A cloud of shad-flies comes aboard; the deck is covered with them, and each seems to propagate there and then. 'They come when the shad are running. They live two days and that's that', we are told. The sun is very hot. We pass a bridge with a vertical-lifting central section, as the banks narrow for the channel. *Kathleen* has distanced us across the lake, but there she is, waiting for the lock. All along the top wharf ships' crews have filled in time painting their ship's name and country: among many we see Cyrillic and Greek characters.

An inland navigation calm descends. *Kathleen* waits; so do we. We see the red-and-white Canadian flag with maple leaf, but what is happening at the lock we cannot see. Our captain strolls forward like a dove from the ark. Charles follows. Seemingly the lock is being refilled. He also reports that *Kathleen* is loaded with Manchester Liners' containers that are probably bound for the Manchester Ship Canal. The lock's red light begins to flash. Action is imminent. *Dinara* from

Jugoslavia emerges from the lock, and we are off, guided by the lock-master's voice on the loudspeaker.

Beauharnois Upper lock again has sector-gates and, as at all locks, a crane stands ready to insert stop-beams in a slot outside the upper gates, should any accident make it necessary to block off the lock. From Upper we move through a massive rock cut into Lower. To our right is an enormous hydro-electric station, making use of the 80ft fall of water and, beyond that, a refinery.

And so out into Lake St Louis, almost an inland sea, cliff-hung to the south, deep blue ahead. A fresh breeze has sprung up. On our left is Ile Perrot and on its far side the old Lachine Canal, lying to the left of the river, leads to Montreal. Coming inwards, Jacques Cartier came to the first rapids of the St Lawrence and, thinking them on the way to China, named them Lachine. We shall now follow the South Shore Canal to St Lambert lock and Montreal.

It is 8pm, and we are in Côte Ste Catherine lock, a spectacle for the locals, who have come in shoals to see the boats go by, and a pleasure to the shad-flies. Away to the left, in the rosy-grey evening, the high rises of Montreal show against the clouds.

All great cities should be entered by water, preferably while standing on deck in the bow of your ship. As we sail slowly along the curving South Shore Canal, Montreal grows up in lights around us. A faint flush lingers from sunset; Mont Royal lies like a lion behind the city, high towers of buildings lit from within shine against the twilight, and the dark canal-wall curves ahead towards the lights. We pass under a great bridge that crosses the wide canal and the much wider river. Cries of seagulls in thousands on the walled banks sound over the water and lead us on to the entrance lock St Lambert, as above the line of poplars bordering the canal the towers of Montreal stand lit up against their mountain. Rail/road-bridges cross the lock at each end. As we move towards it, traffic is crossing the original bridge (its piers the work of Robert Stephenson), at the far end of the lock. The lifting span nearest us rises vertically; once we are in the lock the bridge is lowered behind us, and traffic switched to it ready for the far bridge to be raised for our exit. We have arrived in Montreal.

Next morning we slept happily through to 7 o'clock after our succession of 5am's, and woke to a view of Expo '67, the International Exhibition site across the river, the British pavilion distinguishable by the flag above it. After breakfast a tourist bus arrived at the wharf (Queen Victoria wharf, berth 24) to take most of the passengers, including us, on an outline tour of the city.

The tour itself was not well chosen: for instance, we saw no library or art gallery or museum of history, science or natural history. Moreover, the driver-guide's materialist, sneering tone 'every street corner in Montreal has a bank on one corner and a church on the other', or 'old Mr & Mrs So-and-so live in that house – they need fourteen servants to look after them' and failure to mention any contribution whatever to the city's past or present other than by French-speakers, succeeded in severely prejudicing us against Montreal. We were not alone.

The outward character of the city is in its water and highlands setting. What little is left from before the nineteenth century is to be found in the small preserved, and rather dilapidated, area of Old Montreal by the waterside. The huge city of the nineteenth and twentieth centuries spreads along the St Lawrence and Ottawa Rivers, climbing up to and surrounding the lofty Parc Mont-Royal, and is centred on the streets and squares round the Queen Elizabeth Hotel and the Central Station, where the new underground city of shops and restaurants is linked to the recently-built subway (underground) system. This last derives from Parisian experiments with rubber-tyred cars. One especial pleasure, we had, however, was the distant view from the lower slopes of Mont-Royal of the Lachine rapids.

The ship left Montreal early, and by 7.30 we were going downriver in a strong head wind and bright sun. Houses, little villages and the occasional industrial plant line the banks of the St Lawrence immediately below Montreal, many flying the Canadian flag as well as the Quebecois blue and white. We passed the waiting-room for the Seaway, a line of half a dozen anchored ships, Canadian, Greek, Panamanian, Dutch, awaiting their cue to work up to St Lambert lock. Most of the Seaway traffic being downwards, they are all unladen. We took on a pilot at Montreal. We shall change him for another at Sorel, at the mouth of the Richelieu River, who will take us to the Saguenay River and back.

Except for a couple of showers and a squall on Lake St Louis, the weather has been perfect ever since we left New York. Today, under blue sky laced to the south with fleecy clouds, to the north almost unbroken, we watch the blue-brown water; there is just enough wind to fleck some wavelet tips with white. On deck the feel has changed: this is no longer an inland voyage, but an approach to the sea. Ahead is the Atlantic.

Last night, in the lounge, we tried to pull together some impressions of Americans, for by now we must have talked to three hundred or so; most of them, of course, elderly, as we are, but not all. Most striking is their niceness: always courteous, old-fashioned and delightfully so, always generous of time and possessions, seldom heard grumbling about anything personal to themselves, they make daily life easy under such confined conditions as boat trips necessarily provide. Again, both men and women give off an air of responsibility; almost all, obviously, take responsibility willingly. Such as have retired have moved to voluntary work or part-time jobs. Of the married couples, maybe only the happily married come on such trips as these, but we are struck by the solid contentment with each other of these couples. The total effect is impressive.

Perhaps, however, this high level of social pleasantness and responsibility somewhat dulls intellectual curiosity and practical foresight. We were struck in West Virginia by the difficulty, with National Park officials, of getting past their hospitality and kindness to actually see what we wanted to see, and do what we wanted to do. Again, on these voyages it is noticeable how little preparation nearly everyone has made. Hardly anyone has maps, guides, even knowledge of the route. They are confident that it will all work out – and of course it does, but maybe not at as deep a level for their own knowledge and enjoyment as it could.

A quick exchange of pilots, and the river broadens into Lake

St Peter, then contracts again. We pass the considerable industrial town of Trois Rivières. Hills begin to rise now, and here and there cliffs come down to the river, then fall back. Mile by mile the hills grow into mountains, come nearer, establish themselves as the dominant quality of the scene. Church spires rise from the banks, where there must be dozens of small villages. Our ship's hooter sounds a tune. Enquiry is answered: we are passing the pilot's house, and are greeting his wife.

Ste Anne de la Perard, we are told, is a place for ice-fishing in the winter, little huts being built over holes in the ice. It is hard to imagine, sailing through this sunshine and calm, that the river and the Seaway are blocked by ice for some three months a year in spite of all that icebreakers can do, with very touch-and-go conditions for the last ships out of the Lakes before the freeze-up. Further on, we pass a hill-high house whose owner has the hobby of flying the national flag, and playing the anthem, of each ship that passes. He gave us the full American treatment. The passengers all stood up, as we did as soon as we had recognised the tune. Immediately before, he must have done the same to the Russian freighter we had just passed.

Ahead, the Quebec mountains begin to show on our left: cliffs rise, rocks appear on each side of the buoyed channel. Settlement becomes sparser. Then, far away, the high-rises behind the city (they are in fact the buildings of Laval University) begin to show up, and the white piers of the first bridge. Slowly the hills contract the river. A long railway viaduct of some thirty spans crosses a valley to our left; behind, the far-off Laurentian Hills show through the supports. Ahead, a slender new suspension bridge precedes an older cantilever, at points where the river has narrowed to a few hundred yards. Here the 5-6 knot current under our stern must be running faster still. Sailing-boats play last across as we approach.

The Plains of Abraham lie ahead on a bluff, Wolfe's Cove below, the green roof of the Chateau Frontenac hotel behind. The town of Levis is opposite, across the river, and ahead a great mountain rises grey and distant. Yachts are everywhere, powerboats few. Below the Plains, a line of buildings fronts the river. Above rises the citadel. We swing round Cape Diamond, past the coastguard boats, under the Frontenac. Sharp to the left, and we slide into a small dock. We have arrived in Quebec.

Among the pleasures of boat travel are lights over water. *New Shoreham* is lying at Bassin Louise. Across the St Lawrence lie Levis's scattered lights. On the far side of our basin a coastguard vessel is moored, deck-lights ablaze, the water between us pathed with pink. Beyond that, high above the infrequent lights of the old port, greens grasp up towards the sky – the floodlights of the Chateau Frontenac. High again, rows of lights from high-rises are topped with red aircraft warnings. Nearer and below, a little boat is lined in lights; above, a single floodlight makes a path to our eyes. Water and light: two of God's creations so common that maybe we do not look at them often enough or long enough. Such trips as these give more opportunities to stand and stare.

We did not overly take to Montreal, but Quebec we loved. Maybe this began with the drivers of their respective tour buses, who introduced us to each before we began our wanderings. He of Montreal had no real feeling for the city, but a great deal for money. In Quebec we had a student of French stock, whose history was patchy but who loved his city and liked showing it.

A city built on a hill, overlooking a river, begins with an advantage: Exeter, Durham, Dinan. But at Quebec, what a hill there is, and what a river! The hill not only holds the old town, founded by Champlain in 1608, but spreads behind, past the citadel to the Plains of Abraham. Not the Old Testament character, but Abraham Martin, a farmer, gave his name to one of the world's most famous battles, when Wolfe in 1759, moving silently upriver at night, outflanked the French position by having his men climb the path from Wolfe's Cove to the Plains, and there drew up his army. In a twenty-minute battle Montcalm was defeated, and Canada became British, until in 1867, the first dominion, it became independent Canada. In Quebec there is a joint memorial to Wolfe and Montcalm, who both died of wounds, surely a unique single monument to opposed generals.

Stand at the edge of the Plains, look over the great river,

down to the point from which Wolfe set out, up to the Cove, and remember, as we did, great men and great deeds.

The star-shaped citadel, classic in design though built between 1823 and 1832, was never used. The British had experienced, during the War of 1812 (Mr Madison's War), American attempts to conquer Canada. Though she had repulsed them, she was determined to discourage another try by greatly strengthening Canada's defences. Quebec citadel is one evidence of the effort that was made; later, we shall be seeing the Ottawa River and Rideau Canals, also built for defence purposes in the same period, and visiting another citadel, Fort Henry at Kingston. But things have changed since those days. The frontier is undefended now, and the summer visitors flock to the citadel at Quebec to see the Changing of the Guard, carried out by the Royal 22[e] Regiment of French-speaking Canadians, wearing uniforms derived from those of the British Guards, bearskins and all.

Within its gates, this only walled city north of Mexico is a delight of narrow streets, old dormered houses, good public buildings, little squares, monuments, restaurants, horse-drawn surreys and buggies, and one of the world's best-known hotels, the Chateau Frontenac. Our tour done, and rain coming down in buckets to make rivers of the steep roads, we lunched at La Vendôme on consommé with sherry, lobster grilled, a bottle of white Burgundy, and a delicious whisked-up concoction of egg, cream and brandy. Much as we had taken to United States' ways, it was a pleasure to eat a European-type meal in European-type surroundings. Though the English and the French mostly dislike each other, as they have done for a thousand years and are likely to go on doing for the next thousand, they are both Europeans, and meet at life's nodal points, one of them the table.

Below the hill lies the lower city, small, dilapidated, huddled between cliff and river. House by house it is being restored. One small square, the Place Royale, has emerged, with its 1688 church of Notre Dame des Victoires, full of the grace of simplicity. A model sailing-ship hangs above the congregation. Still extremely unrestored is Rue Sous-le-Cap, claimed the

Quebec 'is a delight of narrow streets . . .'

narrowest street in North America, reminiscent of those in Lisbon's Alfama quarter, where pedestrians have to step into doorways as cars go past.

The rain eased, and back on board in a light drizzle, we had a sound sleep after our lunch, and awakened in time for a captain's party. Tomorrow we were to sail for the Saguenay River some 130 miles further down the St Lawrence. 'May Quebec', we said sleepily as we went to bed, 'long flourish as a jewel in Canada's crown.'

We awoke to sunshine, high fir-forested hills to port, and a yellow Canadian container ship overtaking us. To starboard, the far shore had almost disappeared from sight. Ahead, the hills seemed to become mountains in the mist. We were half way to the Saguenay. Soon we take the channel between the flattish Isle aux Coudres and the hills-becoming-mountains, at a point where a village stands at the foot of a long valley running inland. There is a slight but definite feeling of being on one of the Hurtigrute boats running from Bergen up the coast of Norway between the islands and the mountains. Here and there a log-slide shows, here and there a waterfall or a hill-top farm, a mountain nip in the air. Ahead, the island car-ferry crosses our track.

Past the island, the south bank can only be seen through glasses. The north folds back, treed hills in front, bare mountains behind. Blue sky, white clouds, and sunshine on water and paintwork that makes dark glasses imperative. The passengers sit wrapped up, contented in the sunshine; this is the part of the voyage many have come for, and what a day they have of it! Ahead, two ships bound for the Seaway are creeping up under the mountains. Murray Bay passes, terminus of the railway that has been following us along the shore. We move close under a green-blinking lighthouse on rocky Cap Saumon; beyond, to starboard, is the long, thin Isle des Lièvres; the Saguenay lies not far ahead. A tide-mark runs along the base of the hills, for the St Lawrence is tidal to well above Quebec, but the tide acting more to back up the fresh water than to penetrate it with salt. Suddenly we saw a tide-line caused by a sudden change in depth – a clear demarcation across the river of light water and dark, on this side the river, beyond the sea.

We leave the hills to steer outwards to round a green flashing light, then sharply to port towards the land. A coastguard helicopter swings low a hundred feet above our bow and back again, lands beside the light, takes off again with a large bag hanging below (perhaps the laundry), and flies low south across the river. Up the Saguenay we were to notice that every lighthouse had its helicopter landing pad alongside.

Close in now, we cross over two rough-water bars, on each of which gulls and cormorants were crowded. On the right the village of Tadoussac comes up; on our left the high hills begin to cut off the sharp north-west wind. Perhaps a mile wide, the Saguenay River begins. It is a true fjord, a deep-water mountain-sided inlet of the sea. Tree-covered cliffs rise to perhaps 1,500ft, and here and there a little waterfall slips downwards.

The fjord increases in impressiveness as it unfolds: mile after mile shows no house, no fishing-boat, no cruiser, no bird: hydro-electric lines the only sign of life. There are said to be small white whales but, the more we looked, the less we saw them. Later, however, we did meet one yacht, and see one village, where a valley ran down from the hills into the water, a few fields, and two birds. The Saguenay differs in this desertedness from Norway's fjords and Scotland's lochs, round every bend of which one finds a village or a house, and always boats. And yet, returning later to Tadoussac, we were overtaken to our astonishment by a freighter running empty, for there is indeed a considerable town, Chicoutimi, high up the river.

Canada's fjord-like Saguenay River

We turn at Cape Trinity, some 35 miles from Tadoussac. There, on the left as we approach, high up on a shelf of rock, stands a 25ft white statue of a rather stout Virgin, sculpted by Louis Jobin and erected in 1881. Why, does not transpire, and how he had it erected is a puzzle. At the back of the Virgin's cliff is a sheer rock-face, on the base of which climbers have white-painted their names. The statue high above, we come in right under the rock. Echoes bounce back to our hooter as we turn beneath the great cliff. Here is the *New Shoreham's* farthest point of travel. Far away, the Saguenay (the Indian word means 'where the water comes from') rises in almost circular Lake St Jean, 325ft above sea-level, 140 miles in circumference, and a great place for fishermen.

Tadoussac village, back at the Saguenay's entrance, where after supper we came in to moor overnight, was once a fur-trading and also a missionary post to the Indians. It calls itself the oldest Christian mission in Canada. As we swing out of the river alongside its wharf, its main offerings seem to be a lighthouse, a church and two hotels. In fact, two churches, for near the shore is the tiny white-painted, red-roofed wooden church of 1747, which still carries a bell sent out from France in 1647 for a little church burnt down. By the wharf is a reconstructed early settler's timber house and barn combined, with solid walls, tiny shuttered windows and central chimney. We liked the little place, clustered between wooded points behind its sandy bay, looking up the St Lawrence. A notice, 'Epicier Licencié, 9am à 11pm' reminded us of the much longer shop hours obtaining in North America compared with Britain. In most places one can buy necessaries up to 10pm, and most things to 8pm or thereabouts.

We go sleepily to bed. Now we are for Quebec again, then for the Richelieu River, Chambly, and Robert Legget.

On Tadoussac wharf as we left it at 6am on Wednesday morning were two huge new log-chipping machines, presumably waiting to be taken by water to a pulp mill. The day found us bucketing up the south channel of the St Lawrence (we had come down the north channel) in bright sunlight, but against a stiffish west wind. Beyond the white-capped brownish water lay the long, brownish-blue hills. Away to our right were those we had been close under, yesterday. This is no weather for passengers on deck: half a dozen brave spirits sit in shelter aft; the rest are in the lounge, reading or playing cards, or in the saloon, writing. What a river Cartier must have thought it, once he had realised it was a river, and not an arm of the sea!

After an hour or so the pilot gets us into the shelter of islands and the bucketing becomes motoring, though still our American flag and Canadian courtesy flag flap noisily in the wind. More passengers appear, heads out of companionways to sniff the air like rabbits and make sure all is safe above. It is; they find deckchairs and settle down to read and nap.

In warm but windy late afternoon, westering sun ahead cut by a cloudy trail, we came up to the easterly tip of great Orleans Island, which for many miles divides the St Lawrence. We took the south channel, whence, looking over the low island, we could see the long folded line of the Laurentian Mountains to the north. Beside us on the after-deck sit Fred and his wife. Fred is alleged to be 92, his wife not far behind, yet they are on deck whenever there is something to see, ashore each time the gangway is put down. It hasn't occurred to either of them that they might be too old for such a cruise as this. Two or three other passengers are lame, and one has had bad heart trouble. Yet they too are here, learning, enjoying the scenery, the food and the company. It must take courage to decide to come, more to do it. Houses increase, on the island and the south bank. Ahead are two freighters bound upstream. Our channel swings towards the north, Levis comes up to the left, and there to our right is Quebec high on its hill. We pull in once more to Bassin Louise.

We could write long about our fellow-voyagers, their histories and interests. Here are three glimpses, all from this Quebec evening. A wife turns out to be of Loyalist ancestry: that is, of parents whose ancestors left the newly-formed United States during and after the Revolutionary war, to continue as British people. The British government made grants of land to them in Ontario, Quebec and the Maritime Provinces. Our friend's ancestors settled in New Brunswick and remained there until her father emigrated back to the States in 1922. We told her of the Loyalist celebrations held each year in July in New Brunswick and she, looking for roots, may well find one there.

The French-Canadian pilot came in to dinner, trim, attractive, incurious, compressed. We had an excellent dinner, onion soup, duckling and orange gravy and trimming, sprouts, new-baked bread, not-too-savoury rice and cheesecake. Charles had a bottle of Mateus Rosé on the table. Perhaps that was why the percipient Céline put the pilot opposite to us. The seven Americans at our table gulped, braced themselves and were stifled, but Alice Mary threw her hat into the ring and asked him in English how long the training was to be pilot on this stretch of the St Lawrence. From then on he and Charles took it up unaided by our companions; we had travelled more of his river than he had, but we had also been to Grenoble where he had gone for a week's course. Afterwards, the pilot made a date for the evening with one of the saloon girls (we met them later) and remained attractive, wary, inturned, polite and unrewarding.

Lastly, we went walking with an American wife who turned out to be of French ancestry from New Orleans, with a father whose magnificent name was Romulus Remus César Bech, and memories of Mardi Gras long ago. All Americans have interesting mixed ancestry. The advantages of exploring in a country where you can speak the language are endless, and the real understanding of conversation, chat and jokes comes first.

We strolled out to a cafe in the restored old town with an American woman friend. Sadly, 'bock' meant nothing to the French Canadian waitress, and she'd never heard of 'porto'. We settled for a Canadian brewed beer, and came back to *New Shoreham* to watch floodlit *Sir James Dunn* unloading grain from the Lakes into the silos of the mills that line one side of the Bassin Louise. Our friend's husband, we learned later, wanting to learn the result of the Californian referendum on the property tax, had walked up to the Frontenac, Quebec's biggest hotel and, having glanced at the French language newspapers on sale, had asked the girl at the cigar stand if she had an American paper. 'No', she said. He then enquired where in Quebec he might buy one. 'No American newspapers are sold in Quebec city', he was told.

The weather broke that night. Taking our last stroll we watched black clouds pile up over Levis, and slept to the pattering of raindrops on deck. But Thursday found us running upstream in clearing mist, the slowish *New Shoreham* every now and then being passed by a freighter – as we write, by *Karmalu*, registered in Georgetown, C.I. Research in Webster's *Geographical Dictionary* from the ship's library reveals this as the Cayman Islands, pop. 10,600. A rare specimen.

End-of-cruise lassitude prevails. The bridge and backgammon schools play last games, again library books are skipped to discover the endings, Alice Mary is packing. Ahead at 5pm is the captain's party, which will finish up the voyage's drinks – the bourbon has already gone. One of our two players strums the saloon piano, and the less inhibited perform an elderly but cheerful hop, skip and dance. 'Party' on the *New Shoreham* does not mean what it does on a Fred Olsen or Royal Viking cruise ship. Captain Bob will probably be in shorts, and may have to leave in the middle to take the wheel. As we all know each other well by this time, it becomes a convivial continuation of this comfortable, small-town, shipboard life.

Charles only really misses two things in north America: marmalade and English beer. We would be happy to go on for months floating through America, were it not for Alice Mary's home-made marmalade, Ruddle's County beer , and our own big bed.

Sorel shows up, with a church having two onion-domed spires and enormous grain silos, and we swing to the left out of the main stream into the Richelieu River between moored grain ships and Sorel's twin town of St Joseph, past a floating crane lifting a sunken tug. By a road-bridge we pass a real steamer, the *Lake Transport* of Toronto, seemingly laid up, and blow for a railway swing-bridge. Past a Cuban ship, the *5 de Septembre* and half a dozen other ships at a building yard, and on upriver. We like the change from the great river to something where the banks are nearer. Trees and meadows come close, and we wave to children running down from cottages and caravans (mobile homes).

The Richelieu winds ahead, about the width of the Thames at Richmond. *New Shoreham* is too large to pass the Chambly flight of locks ahead: otherwise we could return to Troy on the Hudson by way of the Chambly Canal, Lake Champlain, and the Champlain branch of the Barge Canal. As it is, we go only to Chambly, some 40 miles from Sorel, where our passengers will be taken by bus to Rhode Island and a new cruiseful brought back.

With the buoyed channel narrowed in places to a width not much greater than our own, the beaten metal of the smooth evening river runs up to our last lock, of 5ft rise, at St Ours (right in the middle of the party). It lies to the left of a wooded island, and has a delightful lock-house with a three-sided pillared verandah, set in neat trees and well-kept lawns smelling of fresh grass. We reckoned we could settle down as joint lock-keepers at St Ours. Was there really a Saint Bear?

The Richelieu above St Ours is beautiful indeed. With its evening lights and reflections, it reminds us of the Thames or, were it to be shrunk in width, the Warwickshire Avon. It looks odd to find a coastguard vessel on a locked river like this, but in the US and Canada the coastguards maintain navigation lights and beacons on all navigable rivers, however far from the sea.

Out of the evening ahead a line of mountains emerges, and slowly moves past to port. We pass two small moored seaplanes, and then two more. Clearly this is not the Thames, still less the Avon. We blow for the road and rail swing-bridges at St Hilaire. Surprisingly to us, the bridgekeepers are still on duty at 8.15pm and the bridges are swung: maybe someone has telephoned. At 9.30, a line of green and red lights winking our channel in the dark across a small lake leads us to Chambly basin at the foot of the staircase of three locks that begins the first flight of the Chambly Canal. To our left humps the old fort, whose log-built predecessor, built as protection against the Iroquois Indians, dated from 1665. We have reached voyage's end, 1,498 miles from Warren.

Chapter 6

Canadian Canal Trails to Niagara

At 9am on Friday, Robert and Mary were on the wharfside. Robert is Robert Legget, author of *Canals of Canada, Rideau Waterway, Ottawa Waterway* and *Railroads of Canada*, as well as being a distinguished geologist and engineer. He and Charles had been pen and personal friends for many years, and now he and his friendly wife Mary were to show us some famous Canadian canals.

American-Canadian Line not being allowed to discharge passengers in Canada, we had to accompany our shipboard friends returning by motor coach to Rhode Island as far as the frontier. Having been formally returned to the United States we drove round the corner out of sight of the immigration officers, transferred ourselves and our luggage to Robert's car, and bade farewell to those many we had become so fond of during the cruise. To avoid giving apoplexy to the frontier staff by going straight back through the same post, we drove through wooded, pastoral Vermont and across the head of Lake Champlain to the next post and returned through that. The customs man could not have been nicer, but the lady in immigration was only interested in how soon we were proposing to leave Canada, not in how long we wished to stay.

Back in the province of Quebec, whose French-only road signs must cause some interesting results from non-French-speaking American drivers, we legged it back to Montreal, over the Seaway at the beginning of the South Shore Canal, and then left along the Ile de Montreal to the pretty old village of Ste Anne de Bellevue. Picturesque in itself, it has the Simon Fraser House for an appetising light lunch. The stone house dates from 1798, and a story goes that while visiting the fur-trader Simon Fraser in 1804, Tom Moore transcribed the Canadian

Boating Song that he had scribbled down while being paddled in a canoe nearby:

Faintly as tolls the evening chime,
Our voices keep tune, and our oars keep time,
Soon as the woods on shore look dim,
We'll sing at Ste Anne's our parting hymn.
Row, brothers, row! The stream runs fast,
The rapids are near, and the daylight's past!

Shades of Charles's preparatory school, where at twelve it had been a class song . . . 'Row brothers, row! The stream runs fast . . . !' Never mind, everything mellows in time, even memories of class-singing when one has no ear and cannot sing in tune, so little so that at choral renderings on prize-giving days Charles was told to move his mouth, but under no circumstances to let a sound come out.

Across the road from the Simon Fraser House is the large Ste Anne de Bellevue lock, lowest on the Ottawa River which is soon to join the St Lawrence and necessary for all craft going up the Ottawa River to pass. Beyond it, the lower-gate recesses of the earlier lock, built in 1843, can be seen. Still earlier was a wooden canoe lock on a different site at the other end of Ile Perrot. High overhead, bridges carry two parts of a main highway, and both Canadian Pacific and Canadian National Railroad tracks.

Above the lock the Ottawa River widens out into the Lake of the Two Mountains. We circled it on by-roads, along the north side of Ile Perrot and then part of the first road to be built between Montreal and Ottawa, now a by-road through the pretty suburbs of Como and Hudson, with glimpses past good houses and flowered gardens to the blue lake beyond. Como is well-named. Then over the car-ferry, ours the only car, to Carillon.

One result of British concern for the defence of Canada after the War of 1812 was the citadel at Quebec. Another was the building of a waterway supply line to the naval base at Kingston on Lake Ontario that did not run along the St Lawrence, itself in its upper section the frontier between the

States and Canada. This supply line was to pass from Montreal up the Ottawa River to what is now Ottawa, and then by the Rideau water line to Kingston. So the former had to be made navigable, while at the same time the Rideau Canal had to be built.

The magnificent Ottawa River – Legget describes it as having an average flow greater than that of all the rivers of England and Wales combined – falls from Ottawa to the St Lawrence, most of it in its natural state through twelve miles of rapid water, the Long Sault. In addition to the lock at Ste Anne de Bellevue, three canals were needed to circumvent the rapids, travelling upwards, the Carillon, Chute à Blondeau and Grenville, and they were built between 1819 and 1834 by the Royal Staff Corps (who in England had built the Royal Military Canal in Kent) under a brilliant engineer, Lieut-Col Henry du Vernet.

The lowest, at Carillon, was through ground so rocky that du Vernet produced what we think was a unique labour-saving solution for a river side-cut. From the upper end of his canal he first lifted his canal through a lock, then ran it level, supplying it by water feeder from the nearby North River, then dropped it by a staircase pair of locks back into the river again. The ruins of the staircase stand by the old lock-house still; beyond, the gate recesses of the larger 1878 lock (part of the 1873–1882 enlargement programme for the Ottawa River locks) show in the approach to what has now replaced and flooded most of the old works, the huge Carillon lock, with vertically rising lower-gate. Built by Hydro Quebec in 1963 as part of a modern generating plan, its 65ft rise overcomes the combined lift of all the old locks, and has left unflooded only the bottom of the Carillon and top of the old Grenville Canals. Alongside the lock the power plant spans the river, backing it up right to Ottawa itself. The spread of water, the high open country, the contrast of wildness with achievement of modern engineering, exhilarates us.

Just below the old lock entrance, the military barracks building of the 1830s now houses the Argenteuil County Historical Museum. Do not miss it, if only for the ship models and photographs of former Ottawa River steamboats, the pictures of the Carillon & Grenville Railroad, and for the Canadian Pacific Railway models. When the steamboat age came in, the three sets of cuts and locks on the Ottawa were too time-consuming for passenger-boats between Montreal and Ottawa. Therefore a special portage railway, the Carillon & Grenville, was opened in 1854 from below Carillon locks to above Grenville. With a gauge of 5ft 6in, isolated from other lines, its one locomotive pushed or pulled two or three coaches along its twelve miles of track until the 1920s. As we stood facing the front door of the museum, we could see in the trees to our right the half-hidden line of the old track.

Through the canal village of Cushing, a small English-looking place with an Anglican church and a delightful double line of small houses under trees, we drove to turn left at the Hotel Manoir, and find the lock entrance of the rebuilt 1877–8 Grenville Canal. One can go beyond, to the end of a small promontory that was once one of its protecting arms. By the bridge stands a stone canal monument, which unhappily gives credit for the original constructions to the Royal Engineers instead of to the Royal Staff Corps. There we said goodbye to the Ottawa River Canals, crossed the river to Hawkesbury, and took the old main road to Ottawa through one of the sudden black cloud and lightning storms that sweep down the valley.

Robert and the assistant manager of the Chateau Laurier hotel in the centre of Ottawa had personally selected the corner turret room on the sixth floor (no 602) that had the best three-way views of the eight-lock staircase that brings the Rideau Canal from Kingston on Lake Ontario down to the Ottawa River. Those locks are historic indeed, for the Rideau and its builder, Colonel John By of the Royal Engineers, in charge of contingents of the Royal Sappers and Miners, created Ottawa – first called Bytown – round this point of meeting.

What a sight they were in the bright evening sunshine as they dropped down the valley to the river, our hotel on one side and, across from it on the facing hill, the Canadian Houses of Parliament with their equivalent of Big Ben. After dinner we stood again at the windows and looked out past city lights to a black line of hills beyond. Above, the evening star and a new moon shone in a fading orange and turquoise sky scattered with small black clouds. Below us the canal and river waters gleamed through the dark trees threaded by the beads of street lights. It was a time of enchantment for such veteran canal enthusiasts as we, and every now and then, undressing, we would peer round the curtains for just one more look.

Next morning we set out to explore, with Robert to guide us. The city centre has the dignity of the chosen capital of a new country with long traditions. Nothing could be more different from Montreal or Quebec, which are provincial cities. No need for puff or self-assertion, but desire to carry out its function towards the citizens of all the confederated provinces.

Its stately Parliament buildings, of the good Victorian Gothic of their time, with a masterpiece of a circular library, stand in open grounds on a key hill point overlooking the river. We were familiar with these from many photographs, but to walk round them was something special. From them spreads out Confederation Park, with many memorials. One is to Colonel By, placed, somewhat to our surprise, beside a pre-1948 fountain from Trafalgar Square, another being in Regina, Saskatchewan. The Rideau Canal as water park and pleasure ground passes through the Park, leading one way to the historic foundation area of Colonel By's locks, beautifully maintained, and on the other right through the developing city to the country beyond. We have seen old canals running through many cities, London, Birmingham, Paris, Amsterdam, Delft – but never have we seen a more beautiful stretch than the Rideau Canal through Ottawa and its environs, or one that has been more imaginatively turned to the uses of today.

We turned along it towards the river. The scene was delightfully gay in the sunshine, with cruisers, canoes, pedalos and the crowded trip-boat *Ottawa Queen* on the water, a big open-air cafe banked with rows of flowers beside the towpath, seats, and sweeps of neat grass shaded with maple trees, people lying under them. Across the canal, and opposite our hotel entrance, is the old railway station, rather oddly turned into a conference centre, the rails having now been banished to a

The Rideau Canal in Ottawa

point two miles from the city centre instead of opposite our (railway-owned) hotel.

Under the main road, we were at the top of the lock staircase that falls amid trees and flowers down a narrow rocky valley to the Ottawa River. Gulls with brown wings with black tips patrolled the canal for tribute. A lock-tender's stone house stands at the top, and half way down Colonel By's Commissariat House of 1827, oldest stone building in the capital city, and now the Bytown Museum. To the right of the valley, reached by walking round the hotel, is Major's Hill park, and in it Colonel By's statue and the site of his house. At the end of the right-hand cliffs, on a knoll, stands a statue of Samuel de Champlain, first European to set his foot here.

In the Museum we saw the replica of By's own surveying instrument, given by Robert Legget, the original having been made in London by the great cartographer John Cary. We were coming out of the Museum when the noon gun boomed, as it has every weekday (10am on Sundays and public holidays) since 1869. The charge is fired from a 9-pounder muzzle-loading gun that dates from 1807.

That afternoon, after we had lunched on the hotel's open terrace that stands above the upper locks, we motored up the canal line into the suburbs. Every winter this long city section of canal closes on 1 November, is partially drained, freezes, and becomes an elongated skating rink for the people of Ottawa, sometimes as many as 50,000 at one time, until it is reopened on 1 May. We saw Dow's Lake, a widening of the canal into a side lake, now a yachting area, then drove through a park that in spring is jocund for miles with tulips still given by Holland each year in gratitude for Canada's hospitality to the Dutch Royal Family during World War II (Princess Margriet was born here). Higher up, past two staircase pairs of locks, is the Hog's Back, where By, coming from Kingston, originally took the canal out of the Rideau River for his approach to the Ottawa. On the right are the canal and two locks, on the left the Hog's Back falls, tumbling and rushing down a narrow rocky defile.

We drove on to the little village of Manotick, where we had tea on the grass under the trees in the grounds of an old wooden mill-house. Nearby stood a wooden carriage-house where vehicles could be left while their owners visited the miller. The stone mill building stood opposite: 'Watson's Mill. Feed. Seed. Feed Cleaning. Custom Grinding. Est 1860'. This old water-driven mill, which utilised the fall from one of Colonel By's dams, has been restored, and now its wheel is grinding once again. Inside is a little museum, with pictures and advertisements of barges and passenger-ships from the old navigation days of the Rideau: others are in the mill-house. The provincial flag of Ontario is red, with the Union Jack in one corner and a shield with the arms of Ontario. It goes well with the Canadian red and white and red maple leaf, and people delight in flying them together – a good practice.

We also found and liked a growing Canadian habit of volunteers running and manning something that serves the public and makes money for charity: the Simon Fraser house at Ste Anne de Bellevue (for nursing funds), the Bytown Museum and, in this case, the mill-house serving teas to help the funds of the local historical society.

We returned past wooden farmhouses back from the road with low-pillared verandahs (porches), comfortable with rocking-chairs, and a notice: 'Cedar Trees for Sale', until we came to triple staircase locks at Long Island, by-passing rapids. To English canal-buff eyes, staircase-locks on a river navigation look odd indeed, but here their chief disadvantages, extravagance in water consumption and delays to traffic, did not apply, for there was ample water in the Rideau River, and Colonel By did not anticipate overmuch traffic. Their chief advantage, cheapness of construction, was, however, very pertinent, for the British Government was paying for the canal, rationing Colonel By to so much expenditure a year. Beside it stands one of By's massive curved masonry dams, the stones, oddly, set vertically.

Back in the hotel, we had a battle with the plumbing parallel to our fearful encounter at Chicago. Here we had the same type of multi-purpose tap. This time it jammed while being turned on at VERY HOT, and Alice Mary shot out of the bathroom, unlike Niobe all steam. We kept the heated flood at bay while Charles dialled for an urgent plumber (Sunday night, of course). He came, laden with tools. He wielded his screwdriver.

'Ah, yes, 'e sometimes stick fast, no?'

'No – yes' we chorused.

The flood subsided. He left. We tried the tap. It was still immovable, though now shut off. Sadly we stood on one leg and then on the other, washing our feet in the basin.

On Monday, with Robert and Mary, we set off by car for a 2½-day exploration of the Rideau Canal and the Trent-Severn Waterway. It was all the time we could spare, but anyone who follows us should allow a week, for they will have to travel far to find two more beautiful navigation routes.

We had seen some of the Rideau already: that day we saw nearly all the remaining locks to Kingston and Lake Ontario. We tried, too, to bring alive in our minds some conception of Colonel By's achievement. Straight out from England, this engineer officer managed, in the years from 1826 to 1832, with work on the ground only possible for part of each year, to build this canal/river/lake route, 123½ miles long, with 47 locks 134ft x 33ft and several substantial masonry dams, through a largely untamed country of woods and swamps, bush and rapids. Two years after the Rideau line was completed, in 1834, the Ottawa River canals were also finished, the sheltered military water route to Kingston became a fact, and the defence of Canada was thereby eased.

Of all the canal works, the jewel is Jones Falls. As you come into the little place, on the left, beside the water and the wooden swing-bridge, is the Hotel Kenney. Have lunch, and as you sit down at your table in the waterside dining-room, there, not a hundred yards away, are the bottom gates of a three-lock staircase that disappears upwards into the woods. Like Hilltop House, the hotel is a joy, for it has long been run by the same family, and for its position.

Jones Falls: 'the bottom gates of a three-lock staircase . . .'

After lunch we climbed up beside the steep staircase to a small lake. At right angles across it is another lock, its great rounded abutments thrusting out into the water. Past that, and past a new one to us, a defensible lock-house, we came to the huge gently curved masonry dam, stones set upwards, that is perhaps Colonel By's greatest engineering work. As one looks now at this part-wooded, part-cultivated land, criss-crossed by roads and dotted with farms, villages, factories and towns, it is almost impossible to project oneself back to his day when, in the case of one man, it took him three days to get from the bottom of the locks at Ottawa to the site of those at Hog's Back, still within the modern city. Here at the Jones Falls dam, the stone was quarried and shaped six miles away, the blocks then dragged down by sled to the water's edge, and brought by barge to the site. We had read about By's great work when Robert Legget had first published *Rideau Waterway*, when to think of standing on it was foolishness: now we were here, and a dream had been fulfilled.

The lake water was deep blue, the trees a deep green, on this really hot June day, as we walked back down the path beside the locks to the car. A chipmunk dashed between bushes, tail up. Through wire-fenced farmland we went, past herds of Hereford or Holstein (we call them Friesian) cows and calves, hay-acres, tall barns built of logs, often roofed with aluminium sheets, lonely houses, or else through dense poplar or spruce woodland, or sometimes cedars, though a smaller tree than we think of as a cedar. Road banks were bright with buttercups and moon-daisies.

We came to the last set of locks at Kingston Mills, again a staircase of three and a singleton, with one of the three blockhouses on the canal set beside it to remind us that the canal was built as a military work. Below the bottom lock-tail ran the Canadian National rail line from Montreal to Toronto and Chicago.

The Rideau, like the other smaller canals, is in the care of Parks Canada. Unlike England, each lock has its own lock-keeper and, this being so, many of the lock areas have been laid out as places of interest in themselves. Printed notices give information about the lock and the waterway, and leaflets are available. There are picnic tables and chairs set in the shade, nicely-mown grass areas to lounge on, plenty of rubbish-bins (trash-cans) and toilets in or by the lock-house. And always the Canadian flag flies from a lockside staff. The canal was, to our minds, an outstanding example of how a historical monument and yet a line busy with pleasure traffic can also be made an amenity, no one purpose over-shadowing the others.

Tired as we were, we couldn't help turning aside just short of the town of Kingston to drive round Fort Henry. When the United States declared war on Britain in 1812 – the Americans call it 'Mr Madison's War' and consider they won it; we 'the War of 1812' and, given that we were fighting Napoleon at the same time, it was at worst a draw, with Canada, the Americans' principal objective, left intact – Fort Henry was begun, as a hastily-built defence work. Later it was rebuilt as a powerful fort whose outlying Martello towers look familiar to English eyes, though built forty years later than those around our own coasts. It was continuously manned until 1891, first by British troops, then after dominion status in 1867 by Canadian troops. Today, Fort Henry is a museum where in the summer gun salutes, marches and drills go on, with in July and August the student-manned Fort Henry Guard doing their nineteenth-century drills.

Kingston had had a lot of rain this day, and in the evening sun the waterside city gleamed and glinted. After much travel in big-scale inland country, this trim port on water stretching to the horizon, with its naval installations, held a sea-frontier character.

We two had a private anniversary to celebrate that evening, and with the Leggets to help us we did, in our Holiday Inn's top floor dining-room looking out over the water of Lake Ontario. A quick evening walk afterwards threw up a good-looking restaurant in an 1844 Fire Hall building, the beautifully designed City Hall of 1848 that for a short time served as the *de facto* federal capital of Canada building until Ottawa was finally chosen, the former railway station beside the water with a Canadian Pacific 4-6-0 locomotive preserved alongside it, and the little Battery Fort in the park nearby.

Next morning Robert drove us round beautiful Queen's University, where once he had taught, and then along the lake road 33 to the intriguing peninsula of Prince Edward County, which stretches over half way back to Kingston along the coastline, and is joined to the mainland by one narrow neck 1½ miles across. We crossed the strait to Glenora by the Picton ferry, first of many names of Wellington's officers. A Loyalist Coach Lines bus was already waiting. Driving across to the southern coast road, we passed through small pretty places where architecture paid little attention to changing fashions but kept a classical tradition simplified to needs. The scenery is on a small scale here, unlike all we have been seeing in Canada – stone quarries, market gardens, cattle farms, woods, beaches thrown up by the lake and overgrown, a little iron-ore railway track crossing and recrossing the road; past a notice 'Jug Milk' and 'D.J's Lunch', orchards and nurseries, we climb gently up to Kanaka Heights and come down to Carrying Place, an old Indian portage point at the neck of the peninsula. Then to Trenton and the mainland.

Just beyond Trenton, the 6-mile lockless Murray Canal with manned swing road- and rail-bridges links the main water of Lake Ontario to the Bay of Quinte through the peninsula neck. We passed 'English Settlement Road', 'Prince Charles Public School', 'Jug City', and stretches of wild blue lupins.

At Trenton the Trent-Severn Waterway begins, a winding and twisting canal-river-lake route that is a joy for its scenery and a gem for canal connoisseurs. It took a record time to build – from 1833 to 1920 – and upon its route are the only two vertical lifts (the Canadians call them lift-locks) ever built in North America, at Peterborough and Kirkfield, and the only currently working inclined-plane at Big Chute. Given that we had a day and a half to explore its 241-mile length from its beginning at Trenton to its end at Port Severn on the Severn River that runs into Georgian Bay which is part of Lake Huron, we could do no more than follow its route as well as we could to see locks and dams as we passed, and visit the special items. Side roads to most are well-signposted.

Charles and Alice Mary on the Peterborough boat-lift

In the canal age Britain built several working and experimental lifts, that is, contrivances for raising and lowering boats vertically, and still has one, at Anderton in Cheshire, to raise boats 50ft from the River Weaver to the Trent & Mersey Canal. There are a number of working examples in Europe, including the huge new one on the Elbe Lateral Canal at Lüneburg near Hamburg.

At Peterborough, two tanks each 140ft long, 33ft wide and 8ft deep, stand side by side, one being at the top of the huge concrete structure when the other is at the bottom. In operation boats enter either or both tanks (as a boat displaces its own weight of water, there is no difference in load). Doors are then slid across the ends of the tanks and the canal to isolate each, after which extra water is added to the upper tank, which is held up by a single vertical post or ram beneath it. The extra weight pushes the ram down into a press filled with water; this is forced sideways into a parallel press, and so upwards to lift the second ram carrying the other tank. The vertical rise between the one water level and the other is 65ft, and the load of one tank is 1,700 tons. Peterborough was begun in 1896 and completed in 1904.

We approached Peterborough lift past a notice that read: 'Peterborough, the Lift-Lock Town'. That, we thought, is the right way to appreciate a canal. Just outside the town we found the great structure, the steel upper tank protruding like a half-opened drawer from its 100ft concrete tower. As we were getting out of the car a cruiser approached. Like an elderly

Peterborough lift at work

rocket Charles was off, cameras swinging, legs twinkling, to watch and photograph the working. It was impressive – about two minutes of actual lifting time once the doors had been shut.

Then on again, the country now rough, very wild and empty, but with many smaller lakes and marinas, to Kirkfield, lesser-known, later-built (in 1907), with more structural steel about it and less concrete, and a lift of 49ft. We had arrived after closing time, and half a dozen boats were already moored at the approaches, waiting for morning.

We had motored nearly 270 miles that day, and were ready for our beds in the Beaver motel near Beaverton, by Lake Simcoe. Round the corner, on the Argyle road, was the Terrace Restaurant, an excellent example of the Canadian wayside eating-place, where we had a good three-course dinner and a bottle of wine chosen from a modest wine list quite as good, and much cheaper, than that of biggish hotels. Naturally, we went back there for breakfast, reckoning that half a grapefruit, cereal, two eggs sunny-side-up and bacon, toast, marmalade, and unlimited coffee would see us on our way ('sunny-side-up', 'sunny' or 'up' means fried eggs not turned; 'over' means turned).

To waterway enthusiasts like us, Big Chute was splendid. The old inclined-plane (marine railway or *ber roulant* in Canada) is an electrically-operated wheeled cradle running on standard-gauge rails which carries pleasure-cruisers dry from one level of the river to another. It has worked easily and efficiently for sixty years or so. It is now to be supplemented by a much bigger affair, a very large cradle running on eight wheels instead of four. This new one seemed nearly ready.

The waterway used to have a second marine railway, at Swift Rapids. There a lock was recently built instead, but here the railway is being kept – because of the sea lampreys. Lampreys, we are told, are not good things for fishermen. They plague the Great Lakes, but have so far been kept out of Lake Simcoe and the interior lakes. Adventurous lampreys might get worked through a lock, but are unlikely to be carried on a fibreglass hull up Big Chute railway. Therefore, no lock.

As at Peterborough, luck was with us. Soon after we had

Big Chute marine railway

arrived, a cruiser came to the bottom landing-stage. Charles pounded down the staircase as the cradle followed him along its rails into the blue water below, bright in the hot sunshine. The cruiser floated on to it, the cradle rose dripping, and two men, on galleries one each side, tightened girths that held the boat stable. Quietly it rose up the track and disappeared over the summit, to slip gently into the water above. Only then did Charles use his last picture, and had to change his film, so much were the waterways gods with us. The principle of the new railway is the same, except that whereas on the old one the boat is tipped up as it rises, which can't be altogether good for the china, on the new, the cradle can be kept more or less level during the transfer.

A brief call at Port Severn, last lock towards Georgian Bay, just so that we could say that we had seen the waterway's two ends, and on to Toronto's riot of expressways and high-rises, where we sadly said goodbye to our good friends and guides, Robert and Mary Legget. Wishing we had time to ride the single-decker trams (streetcars) and try out the new pattern of CLVR (Canadian Light Rail Vehicle) just coming into service, we caught our first transatlantic express bus – Grey Line Coaches' Niagara Falls in two hours non-stop. Comfortable, fast, we sped through places only not anonymous because we had a road map, west through Burlington to the end of Lake Ontario, round it, and east back again on the south shore. Over the Welland Canal on an elevated road-bridge, with a glimpse of a ship in the staircase locks on the escarpment, and into the town of Niagara Falls. A few minutes later we staggered into our room at the Sheraton Brock Hotel.

Imagine a room on the eleventh floor, with a balcony. It is filled with a distant roar: outside, to the right, the rock-broken American falls. Beyond, a cloud of spray rises from the Horseshoe Canadian falls. In front is the international bridge across the Niagara River, and across it is the United States. Below, cars pass the control barriers at a rate of half a dozen a minute. Niagara Falls! Honeymoon Capital of the World, the notices say, and that's all right with us. But dinner comes first.

For our eleventh floor we had to change lifts at the ninth. We read in our room brochure of the Rainbow Dining Room 'at the top of the Sheraton-Brock' and happily pressed the lift-button marked 12R, the highest. We emerged onto a bedroom floor just like ours: 'R' must mean roof. The only other 'R' was 10R, so we pressed that, and arrived in the kitchen, between the washing up and the trash-cans. Heaven knows what that 'R' stands for. All that was left was 10, so we tried that, and triumphantly arrived where the restaurant's picture windows give broad views of the falls as one eats. Wonderingly, we fell into bed and slept the clock round. And in the morning found that the bath was long(ish), and had two clearly marked taps 'H' and 'C', and a plug. Hallelujah!

We got up to a late room-service breakfast eaten in view of both falls, and went out to fulfil a great-grandson's duty. In 1785 Charles's great-grandfather Joseph Hadfield visited the

The American and Horseshoe Falls from our bedroom window

United States, where he met George Washington at Mount Vernon and then journeyed by water up the Hudson River, through Lake Champlain, and so to Montreal and up the St Lawrence to Niagara. There, being of an enquiring turn of mind, he got down under the Canadian or Horseshoe Falls into the Cave of the Winds:

> I had heard of this body of water being so great as by its density to become opaque. I was determined to prove it. I entered boldly and might advance from 15 to 20 feet or a little more. I did remain long enough to ascertain it, for I found the heat to be so intense my breathing became difficult, and in a violent perspiration I sought the opening and was happy to emerge freely again. I must here remark that notwithstanding I had the full power of the sun's rays acting on the body of water all was dark, as if I had been entombed in a cavern.

So we set off for the scenic tunnels of the Canadian falls. Passengers are provided by efficient staff with oilskins and Wellington boots. Then groups of rubberised enquirers descend over a hundred feet in lifts to tunnels in the rock. One leads to a platform just beside the edge of the falls. Another runs to two exits right under the water, where one can stand close beneath the roaring, tumbling mass. The ground shakes with the water's power, and natural light is little, for great-grandfather Joseph was quite right: one cannot see through the water. As we walked away after being restored to daylight, we watched others being taken on a funicular railway down to river level to dress again in oilskins and embark on *The Maid of the Mist* (all the boats have the same traditional name) to voyage through the spray and tumbling waters to the very foot of the falls, be held there for two or three minutes, then swing breathtakingly away down the swiftly swirling river to the landing-stage. 'We'll be there', we said, 'but not today!'

Before we could voyage in her, we had two canal visits to pay.

Whereas the St Lawrence Seaway is a canalised river, the Welland Canal is a true ship canal, an artificial cut from one end to the other, taking the same ocean-going freighters and lakers that use the St Lawrence. Put like that, it sounds easy, but a great escarpment over 300ft high rises along the Lake Ontario shore. The canal has to climb over that to Lake Erie, rising by the height of Niagara Falls plus the remaining fall of the Niagara River. Conceived by William Hamilton Merritt, the first Welland Canal was built by the Welland Canal Company and opened in 1829: the present Welland is the fourth, built in 1932 (though straightened since), 26 miles long and 27ft deep with 8 locks 859ft long by 80ft wide. Merritt's canal had 40 locks, each 110ft x 22ft. One of the world's great waterway sights is of a ship in the huge central staircase of three locks that climbs the steepest part of the escarpment. Only Panama is comparable.

The Seaway Authority were kind enough to show us the canal – and even to provide a British ship for us to photograph in lock 2 – and also the fascinating control-room, where a few men watching television screens, listening to short-wave radio and telephones, reading teletype, control the movement of ships in and out of locks, the distance between them, the places to pass, not only in the fine weather we were then having but at night, in rain, fog and, as the end of the navigation season approaches, usually in December, iced-up conditions. Even preventing fools from being foolish, for as we drove along the canal two pleasure-craft waiting to enter a lock were moored far ahead of the board which marked the waiting limit. About to leave the lock was a freighter, and it only needed a gust of wind to blow her stern to one side to reduce both craft to matchwood in seconds. Our guide radio-telephoned control, reported them, was instructed to move them, and did so. Disgruntled, they towed themselves backwards to safety.

For much of the working year, which begins again in March when the ice melts, the Welland Canal operates at near capacity, depending upon the men in that control-room to deal with all the many things that can happen to big ships in a channel only twelve inches deeper than the maximum permitted draft, and not much wider than two ships' widths.

The Welland Canal runs entirely in Canada, west of Niagara Falls, from Port Weller on Lake Ontario at the northern end to Port Colborne on Erie at the southern. In the other direction, across the United States border, lies Lockport, its very name telling why we sought it out. When the first Erie Canal was opened in 1825, the parallel staircases (combines) of five locks each, lifting the canal 66ft, were a wonder of their time. One of the flights remains today, the gates removed, but still there; where the second flight once climbed the hill, the staircase pair of locks of the New York State Barge Canal stand instead.

'Lockport, to see the canal locks?' said the taxi-driver. 'If you want to see locks, I'll take you to the Welland Canal.'

'Been there,' we countered triumphantly. He rang his headquarters by radio: 'How do I get to Lockport?' he asked. (It was only 25 miles away.) They told him. We crossed the great steel toll-bridge that takes the road over the Niagara gorge to the States.

'Going to Lockport to see the canal locks', Charles told the customs officer. He looked at our British passports, stamped with waterway imprints from the Douro to the Danube, raised his eyes to heaven, and waved us on.

We ran past Brock's monument (not our hotel, the other one, commander of the British forces hereabouts in the War of 1812) and past the neat rows of vines in the wineries of New York State. It is rich land, and occasional mansard-roofed wooden barns tell that it has been well farmed for a long time. 'Replacement heifers, Trefoil Seed and Hay', said a notice on one of them. Further on, beside the road, a board advertised the 'Deputy Sheriffs Association Annual Stag Picnic', and our imaginations played with its possible goings-on as we ran into Lockport.

One cannot miss the Barge Canal, and in the town centre is the Lockport Walkway; it leads to the two flights of locks, the old and the new. Look from the natural basin with its 100ft slopes at the bottom of the old flight, up past the iron railings and the steep steps, to the sky beyond the steep-sided rock cutting, and know why men thought it a wonder of its time, and the editor of the local Rochester paper wrote on 28 June 1825 'a work which will probably remain for ages as a monument of American genius and American patriotism'. And what a time it was, for the year before had seen the Welland Canal begun, and the year following was to have the initiation of both the Rideau Canal and the Pennsylvania Main Line.

There, at Lockport, we ended our canal pilgrimage. At the Canadian customs post Charles produced our passports:

'We've just been to Lockport', he said.

'What did you buy there?'

'Nothing – we went to look at the canal locks.'

He gave Charles a long, cool stare; then Alice Mary; then the driver. Raising both eyebrows until they disappeared into the peak of his cap, he waved us on as one who lets circus elephants through his barrier.

Our taximan, having by now entered into the spirit of our dottiness, took us round to see the Spanish Aerocar, the cable railway that has spanned the whirlpool below the falls since 1916, the floral clock, the pad where the sight-seeing helicopter takes off, and the impressive canals that carry Niagara River water from above the falls to the hydro-electric power stations, for power has been generated here for over a century. We parted with promises to meet again, for he is to drive us to Buffalo airport.

It was warm, with mist hanging in the air, when we joined the queue for the *Maid of the Mist's* run below the falls. The funicular car, Swiss-made in 1956, went down the gorge side under trees, honeysuckle bushes and sweet rocket on each side. At the boat we were handed black oilskins to agree roughly with our sizes (on the American side of the river the oilskins are yellow, presumably to prevent illegal exit via the boats from one country to the other). Fortunately we never cause doubts – the man reaches for the longest for both of us.

We make straight for the bow, where we hold on to a central rail. Others crowd along the deck and in the stern, Canadian newly-weds, American families white and black, Oriental groups, swarthy unidentifiables, and two English. The boat sheers over to the American falls, and spray begins to blow across us. Jutting rocks down the face of the falls cause channels of water to rebound and appear to rise continually in masses of foam against the pouring, overwhelming flood. Seagulls glide on the strong updraught from the water's rush.

We move slowly upriver, waiting for the right moment to pass the returning boat, for the swirling currents in water 180ft deep are much to be respected. So close are we that the wall of thundering green water and white foam begins to shut out sound and raise excited spirits. Another *Maid* comes through the mist round the great jut of the Canadian Horseshoe falls, and we move on into rough water and a world suddenly contracted to a green-grey half circle of massive, green and white water, a roar fierce enough to stop all sense of sound and intoxicate the spirits, and drenching, gusted spray that fills the shoes and drives against one's face as one clings to the rail, the only thing left on man's scale. Talk of power, of majesty, of myth – go close below Niagara. Is Nature tamed, and this earth too small for man? Go in an open boat below Niagara.

Too soon our boat began to turn, heaving strongly as she struggled in the rushing current. We came out of the fierce wild lashing into sunshine and calm, and made downriver past the American falls to turn and work quietly up to the landing-stage. Great-grandfather Joseph would have loved it.

The area on the Canadian side facing the American and Horseshoe Falls, and for long stretches above and below, is a model of how to manage a heavily-visited beauty spot. The answer has been in unified control. The Niagara Parks Commission, a body which dates from 1887, provides paths, gardens and seats, fountains, picnic places and trash-cans. It offers milkshakes and beer, snacks and four-course dinners, funicular railways, Viewmobiles (road trains), scenic tunnels and souvenir shops. The result is a marvel of beauty and tidiness, all consciously low-key, subordinated to the mighty falls themselves. We would not have believed that we could sit on a cafe seat, as we are doing now, several hundred people in sight, and see, quite literally, not one piece of litter, nor one notice that says 'Prohibited'. The crowds, clearly, are subconsciously affected by this orderliness to be themselves orderly and easy-going. Whoever the Commissioners may be, we salute them. They will, we are sure, feel quite at home when they reach the Elysian Fields. *O si sic omnes!*

This is one Niagara. But when your thoughts turn to entertainment, you have only to walk a short way to the Clifton Hill Tourist Area. Never have all tastes been so splendidly catered for. In one short street there is Tussaud's English Wax Museum ('licensed by Tussauds of Blackpool, England'), with the Biblical Wax Museum next door. There's 'Come in and try our Bed of Nails', the Castle Dracula Museum complete with window corpse, the House of Frankenstein Museum ('Thrills and Chills in Living Animation'), Houdini's Magical Museum, and Ripley's Believe It or Not Museum ('Eccentric? Roman Poet Virgil gave his pet fly a burial costing $100,000. Now in procession inside').

You can have a computer portrait of yourself in one minute, picture yourself going over the falls in a barrel, or 'Become a Celebrity – Have your Name in a Niagara Falls Newspaper' ie have a specially printed headline crediting you with some exploit connected with the falls. If your mind turns to refreshment, there is an 'Authentic English Pub' or a shop that sells 'Icy Cold Slush'; if to a honeymoon in Honeymoon City, one motel offers water beds, another bridal suites.

We must return to Niagara Falls: Alice Mary wants to see herself going over the falls in a barrel, Charles to try a water bed. And we must check up on that pet fly of Virgil's – it wasn't the impression of him we were given at school.

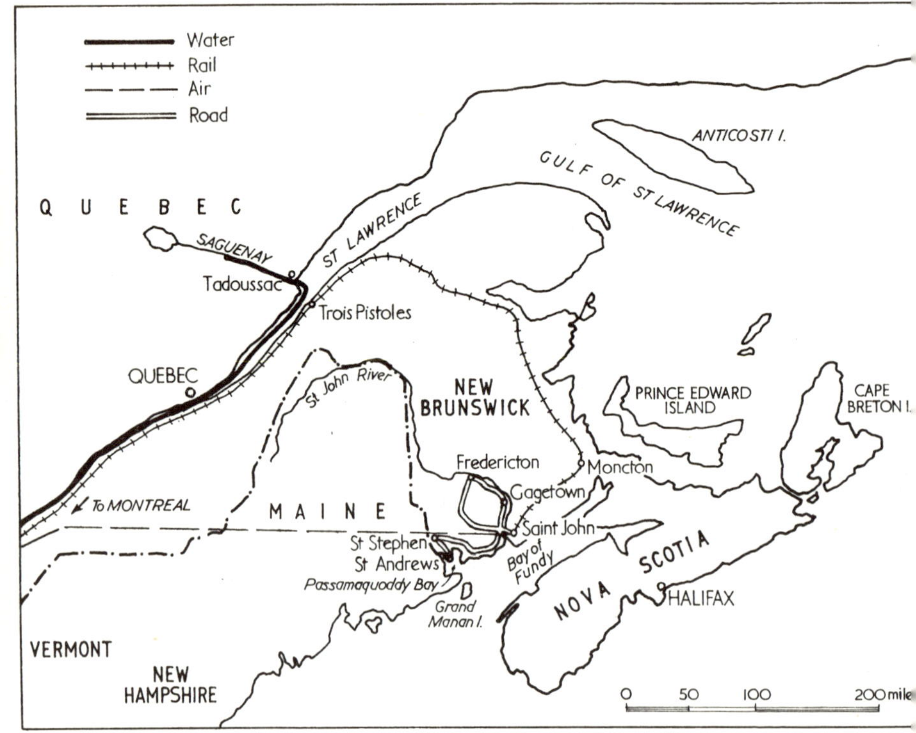

Chapter 7

Railway Coda: New Brunswick to New York

Our friend Darren the taxi-driver was exact to time to take us to Buffalo airport. He chose to drive us by way of the parkway that runs past the falls and on beside the Niagara River to Lake Erie. This could have been one long ribbon development, but the Niagara Parks Commission has kept houses, motels, marinas, shops and whatnot under control, so that green-shaded, blue-watered views open up one after the other all the way to Fort Erie, the small Canadian town that faces American Buffalo across the river. Two signs in Fort Erie amused us: 'Denture Therapy Clinic' and 'Yoga Boutique'.

Darren took us on to old Fort Erie itself, still flying its British flag where river meets lake, and then over the high Peace Bridge into Buffalo, with a glimpse of where the barge canal enters the lake. We saw it again, two vertical flood-gates raised, from the window of our Allegheny British BAC One Eleven as we circled into Rochester, where on the first Erie Canal an eleven-arched stone aqueduct 802ft long had been built over the Genesee river, one of the canal's major works. Then north to Montreal to change planes and let Air Canada take us down to the lights of Saint John, principal port and largest town in New Brunswick, where we were to spend some ten days with our son Alec, his wife Ann, and their two small daughters.

The Maritimes (New Brunswick, Nova Scotia, Prince Edward Island) show a Canada very different from that of Ontario or Quebec, one largely rural, heavily wooded, comparatively poor, with only scattered industry. There's a different feel about Saint John (so called to distinguish it from St John's, the capital of Newfoundland).

It is the kind of place we like, 'for blow, not for show', as Charles's mother used to say of pocket handkerchiefs. Streets of pleasant, slightly romantic-looking wooden houses are mixed up with ships in the growing general and container port, bits of industry, power plants, churches, rocky cliffs, museums, an oil refinery and deep-water oil terminal, and patches of woodland, while all around is water, in Saint John harbour one side of the old town and Courtenay Bay the other, in the St John River that runs into the harbour and in its tributary the Kennebecasis that runs round behind the town. And if you climb to Fort Howe, you can see Nova Scotia's shore low across the Bay.

Saint John stands on the Bay of Fundy, which has the greatest rise and fall of tide in the world, some 28ft at Saint John and 52½ft at its head. Hence the reversing falls where harbour meets river, an oddity where the river current runs over rocks to the sea at low tide, and the tide runs over the same rocks up the river at high tide.

As we had motored along the Ontario coast from Kingston to Trenton we had been made aware of the other side of the American Revolutionary War – the exodus during and at the end of it of the Loyalists who had fought with the royal army or supported the union of Britain and her colonies, for many plaques and place-names along that shore commemorated them. On the one hand *non grata* with the new authorities, who had in many cases confiscated homes and possessions, on the other they wished to go on living on British territory. Some had gone to Florida, which was then British, or home to Britain, but some 50,000 went to Canada; many to Ontario, some to Quebec, but many also to what was soon to become New Brunswick.

The St John River had been named by Samuel Champlain in 1604, and acquired its first French fort in 1631. Coming under British rule when the French ceded Canada at the end of the Seven Years' War in 1763, a trading post was established at Saint John the following year, and Fort Howe built in 1778. Major Studholme's restored wooden fort still stands above the harbour, flanked by guns (and, comically, stocks and a pillory) to defend the place from American attacks. And then, in May 1783, as the American War ended, the first fleet of twenty ships brought more than 4,000 people from the

New York area to disembark at Market Slip in Saint John. Two more fleets followed, till some 9,000 settlers had arrived from the American states to begin a new life in wilder country than they had left, themselves only a fraction of the many that came to New Brunswick and Nova Scotia as a whole.

In so far as Government could help, the Loyalists coming to Canada were efficiently aided. Each settler was granted land, much of which had to be bought from the Indians, with more for sons and daughters, and also given tools, seed and food rations for some years until he had established himself – an efficient piece of administration for those days, worked out by Evan Nepean, head of a branch of the Home Office in Britain administering the colonies (a town in Ontario commemorates him) working with the Governors-General of Canada, Sir Frederick Haldimand till 1784, and then Sir Guy Carleton.

A whole series of events followed. In 1785 Saint John was made a city by royal charter, the first in Canada, and started its own newspaper, and in the same year New Brunswick was carved out of Nova Scotia and made a province. By the early 1800s, backed by great forests and the energy of its new settlers, Saint John had become a major shipbuilding and trading city. Ever since then Loyalist tradition has been strong, for many of the names on the tombstones in the old Loyalist burying ground off King Street are those still known in the city. In July of each year there are the fun and games of the Loyalist Days, with processions and bands and dressing up in eighteenth-century costume. Though too early for the Days, we acquired a Loyalist dollar, specially-minted for the first time, and legal tender within the city during the summer.

From the tourist office the visitor can get 'The Loyalist Trail' leaflet, and follow sites round the city centre. One stop is a 'must', at the clapboard Loyalist House, finished in 1817 by David Daniel Merritt from New York, which, outside and in, is still much as it was then, furniture and all. Owned now by the New Brunswick Historical Society, parties are lovingly guided round by a present-day Merritt, and shown not only the house's major beauties, such as its staircase, curved doors, the superb woodwork of its furniture, but the little things that were

Saint John's two-storeyed bandstand

then part of daily life – such as the formidable skates. Charles reared up at the name Merritt, for he who had promoted the first Welland Canal was of the same family.

In King Square, which seems to be laid out in the pattern of a Union Jack, we liked the recently-restored two-storeyed bandstand – ornamental pool below, band above, and atop the roof a cornet, for the bandstand was given by the City Cornet Band in 1909 and named after King Edward VII.

When we want to know what the locals really eat, use, wear, we visit the local market. Saint John's, a producers' market, was full of good things, but especially lobsters, blue-black in tanks or scarlet on slabs, fresh fish, cheeses and maple syrup. A stand displayed children's toys made by Micmac Indians. There were baskets of fresh strawberries – we bought two – and piles of dulse, bagged and loose. Dulse is a local delicacy, a seaweed, the locals alleging that the habit of seaweed-eating was brought from Scotland. We felt absolved from trying it; we had once eaten laver in Cornwall, and the impression it left proved indelible. There were also heaps of fiddleheads, a curly-shooted edible fern that grows wild hereabouts and is picked in June. Fiddleheads are a New Brunswick 'thing'. To mention them is a certain opening gambit at a party. That they grow and are eaten elsewhere in Canada is, naturally, ignored by all true New Brunswickians.

When you have followed the Loyalist trail, and maybe tried dulse and fiddleheads, go find the beavers at Beaver Lake, where Ernest and Nancy Mickelburgh (Ernest comes from Streatham) maintain a beaver refuge. Take route 111 to the airport, and then 820 for 15 kilometres to a side road marked 'To the Beavers'. The way runs by Loch Lomond, blue water backed by long grey mountains and spreads of wild blue and white lupins, clover, buttercups, lilac and the carraway plant that looks like fool's parsley. Beside the road are loads of cut timber stacked for the pulp mill lorries.

Beavers like carrots (and apples), sliced, and when Mr Mickelburgh called 'Come on, Charlie', a nose across the pond parted ripples as it swam from its lodge. Out climbed Charlie, sharp little whiskered face with long front teeth, tiny ears, and clouded pupils large in small eyes, long-clawed small forepaws, big webbed back feet, and long, broad, thick unfurred tail. He stood up against the wire fence, gently took a slice of carrot, and allowed himself to be stroked and photographed. His wife had had four kits a few days before, and was not at home to callers. But two younger beavers appeared, anxious for carrots and attention. Across the pond a bullfrog boomed. Ernest Mickelburgh pointed out quite enormous tadpoles.

A beaver's tail is very odd. It has no fur like the rest of him, but is rubbery. He uses it for support when engaged in his usual activity of sawing wood to make dams to maintain a tolerable water level for a comfortable home; but also for propulsion when swimming and, by smacking it on the water, a means of warning.

The evening was enchanted: the pond; the beavers; our 3-year-old grand-daughter feeding them carrots; the old man who knew so much about them; the distant bullfrogs; and around, silence, woods and water and a fading sky.

We drove along the coast road from Saint John for 70 miles to St Stephen at the border of New Brunswick and the American state of Maine in a day of alternating mist and sunshine. In the naturalness with which spruce-covered hills, cottages and little villages are mixed with arms of the sea glimpsed, paralleled, crossed, it reminds us of Norway – only the ferries are missing on this road. But though Norway has the same flowered verges, she has not the great swathes of wild lupins that now, in late June, spread along these roadside banks. But, oh to see a porcupine! Sadly, we passed two little roadside corpses, but never glimpsed a live one.

St Stephen is a jolly rather haphazard border town beside the St Croix River, where the firm of Ganong's Chocolate is credited with having invented the chocolate bar. Our day was made by seeing, astride a first-floor (Canadian second-floor) chimney, vigorously wielding a brush, a chimney sweep in black top-hat and frock-coat. When later we saw him on the ground, we saw also blue jeans and a young, cheerful face.

On our way back we turned aside to the pretty seaside town of St-Andrews-by-the-Sea on Passamaquoddy Bay – one of a number of wonderful Indian names that inspired a poem, 'In New Brunswick you'll find it', which begins:

Sweet maiden of Passamaquoddy
Shall we seek for communion of souls
Where the deep Mississippi meanders
Or the distant Saskatchewan rolls?
Ah, no, in New Brunswick we'll find it,
A sweetly sequestered nook –
Where the swift gliding Skoodawabskooksis
Unites with the Skoodawabskook.

(*How to Brickle*, quoting *The Brickline*,
Omega Management Services)

St Andrews is a Loyalist town. We've probably seen more Union Jacks flying here and hereabouts in two days than one would see in Britain in a month. It was not a surprise, therefore, that the old blockhouse was flying the Union Jack beside the Canadian flag. Or that its streets, as well as King and Queen, are given George III's children's names. Look at the delightful little place from the end of its pier, which has a licensed lobster pound (New Brunswick has two short lobster-fishing seasons, but lobsters caught then can be kept alive in such tanks until wanted – Alice Mary high in the queue).

On our way back to Saint John, we reluctantly passed the signpost for the ferry to Grand Manan Island, Robert and Mary Legget's favourite summer island, Canadian though off the coast of Maine. The drive was pure pleasure. Late afternoon sunshine glittered on lakes and sea inlets between spruce woods in fresh summer growth, and brightened the little painted timber houses and small barns built at intervals along the road facing the water. Lupins, buttercups and tall marguerite daisies, blue and white wild iris in swampy patches, caught the eye all the way. Suddenly, perhaps at a small valley, a cloud of mist hung over low hills and in the woods, and all was veiled. A few minutes, and the brilliance returned. The scene had a continuing freshness in buildings and scenery which without having to be striking was always delightful.

On Sunday we went to Trinity Church, whose congregation dates from the Loyalist landing in 1783, and church building from 1879, two years after the great fire that destroyed much of the wooden town. It has a curious treasure: a wooden carved royal coat-of-arms that dates from about 1714. It seems at first to have been carried around as an army standard; then it was put up in Boston's Council chamber until the revolution, whereupon it was rescued by Edward Winslow and sent to his Harvard contemporary Ward Chipman, one of the Loyalists at Saint John, Winslow saying that 'They (Lyon and Unicorn) . . . have suffered and are of course refugees, and have a claim for residence at New Brunswick'. Rescued from the burning church in 1877, it now hangs beneath a bust of Queen Victoria. Another recorded treasure is the set of antique communion

A.I.A.—K

silver given by George III in 1790.

Trinity Church is an outpost of Devon. The vicar, Mr Legassick from Kingsbridge, preached powerfully in a Devon accent (thinly overlaid with Canadian) that brought back to Charles many a Devon churchgoing from his boyhood, for his mother's family, the Fulfords, have lived long in Devon. Mr Stone, the verger, was from Bradninch, and the first memorial window we looked at was to the Sturdees of Topsham. The church's foundation stone was laid by John Medley, Bishop of Fredericton, New Brunswick and first Metropolitan of Canada, also from Devon – and Charles's great-great-uncle. Indeed, Charles has brought off a curious ecclesiastical double, for his grandfather, Joseph Hadfield's son Octavius, was Bishop of Wellington and first Primate of New Zealand.

If only steamboats had still been running on the St John River, longest on the Atlantic seaboard, rising in Maine and running north to south down the whole depth of New Brunswick, and tidal for eighty miles. The first, the *General Smythe*, was launched back in 1816, and the last, the *D. J. Purdy*, worked into the 1940s. We had therefore to see by car what the locals call 'the Rhine of America', when not referring to the Rhine as 'the St John of Europe'. New Brunswickers do not suffer from backwardness in coming forward.

Outwards we took the direct road over the hills to Fredericton, the provincial capital, a neat and comfortable place beside the lawn-bordered river. We went chiefly to pay our respects to John Medley, who arrived as first bishop with plans, drawn by Frank Wills, for a cathedral in his pocket, though why this bishop from St Thomas's, Exeter, should have had plans based on Snettisham church in Norfolk seemed odd to us. Starting in 1845, he had the large-parish-church-sized cathedral built by 1853, the first new one to be built by the Anglican communion – all the older ones having been inherited at the Reformation. There the old gentleman was, inside his cathedral in marble effigy, with a shrewd, kindly, rural face: but he himself lay outside, at the east end, next to his wife, whose ghost is said to haunt the cathedral – maybe she thinks that with all the Anglican women's activities she organised, she

Fredericton cathedral, its plans based on Snettisham church, Norfolk

should have an effigy too.

Fredericton is Beaverbrook town. The hotel is the Lord Beaverbrook, and down the road is the Beaverbrook Art Gallery, with his collection of pictures, including some Churchills: sadly, it was closed on Mondays, along with much else in Canada and the States. We paid our respects to the Legislative Assembly building and the nice new Playhouse (*The Norman Conquests* running, *Table Manners* coming), but were puzzled by an old people's home run by The International Order of the King's Daughters and Sons. That was a new one to us. Nearby was an Indian totem pole.

On our way back we took the River Road, which winds along beside the St John, through old villages and settlements that owe their beginnings to the days when the river was navigated. One such was Gagetown, older houses (like 'Fred's Shoe Repairs', window full of workboots) and a little marina by the water, newer and bigger ones behind on higher ground, where we also found the Gagetown Apple Cooperative, for this is orchard country. At Queenstown great views begin to open up, of hills, lakes and the broad river. This stretch between Saint John and Fredericton doesn't at all resemble the Rhine, but it is remarkably like Scotland with a touch of Norway thrown in.

At Hampstead, where the river turns into the Long Reach that took us back in memory to Loch Ness, we saw English dog-roses in the hedgerow between the houses built high above road and river. Then, at Westfield, where the River Road meets Highway 7, along which we had driven to Fredericton, we turned aside to cross the St John on one of a pair of cable-ferries. Waterway buffs are also by nature ferry-riders. Westfield was a good one, but further on, past a splendid wooden covered bridge over Milkish Creek (covered against winter snow) and the sad sight of a laid-up river passenger-steamer (*Kingfisher VII* of Montreal), we came to the village of Bayswater, and then the Romeo and Juliette (sic) ferry at Somerville, crossing the wide and tidal Kennebecasis River. This was a real long-run ferry with an overhead navigation bridge, radar, an anchor, and a pier to prevent the ferry swinging on the tide.

It ran on a timetable that everyone knew but us. For twenty minutes we gazed hungrily across the glistening blue water at the ferry sitting on the other side. Then cars began to arrive

> And thick and fast they came at last,
> And more, and more, and more.

Full up, we sailed – no less impressive word will do – for the other shore some two miles away, where we motored past the moorings of the Royal Kennebecasis Yacht Club to find ourselves back in the suburbs of Saint John. What a day it had been, of warm sunshine, of Fredericton's dignified houses in calm streets and spired riverside cathedral, of motoring through high wooded hills, past neat wooden cottages, and everywhere glimpses, views, delights of water, great spreads of water! Maybe we two were steamboat crew in our previous incarnation, and will be beavers in our next.

We had flown to Saint John from Montreal; we decided to return by overnight Canadian National train, though we had no real idea of its interest. From Saint John's small, functional, efficient CN station we caught the 8.20pm connection to Moncton, a two-car diesel train of the high, wide, roomy size the North American loading gauge makes possible, our heavy luggage having been booked through to Montreal. VIA, the Canadian version of Amtrak, now operates the passenger services of Canadian National and Canadian Pacific, but with the difference from Amtrak that CN is already government-owned.

Track goodish, train fast and reasonably well filled, we left Saint John in the characteristic fog, but soon came out into clear evening air as we ran up the valley of the Kennebecasis River, at first immensely broad, then narrowing as we passed into land that could have been part of England. No wonder the locals called the half-way town Sussex. Our hooter bellowing for the frequent level crossings, overhead bridges being almost unknown, we ran through the gathering darkness in rural lightlessness, broke only by a faint gleam from groups of farmhouses. Coming into Moncton at 10.05, the train conductor came along to lift down passengers' luggage from the racks and take the heavier pieces out to the coach platform with old-fashioned courtesy that carries no thought of a tip.

Moncton station, again, was small, new, functional and efficient. The air was still warm, and we stood on the platform until, punctual at 10.25, the Montreal train came in, headlight glaring, bell ringing, painted in the new VIA colours of blue with yellow bands. We had booked a bedroom, and were shown to a little blue-carpeted sitting-room some 6ft by 8ft, with two armchairs, a basin with folding table top and triple mirror above, iced water and a cache of paper cups, a separate toilet closet, a small hanging space and shoe compartment, and shelves with fiddles just where one wants them, by the bunk. Facing us, a battery of switches controlled an electric fan and four sets of lights. Another switch fixed the air conditioning, and there was an attendant button and a razor connection.

As we left Moncton at 10.45, the red-coated attendant came to make up our bunks, so we moved to the adjoining dining-car to drink Moosehead beer and chat to the chief steward about his war-time and more recent visits to Britain, and listen to tales, as real to him as if they were yesterday, of moving Canadian troops across Canada for embarkation for the last war, the train lounges stripped for benches, and of 'huge copper pots' in the kitchen. Sometimes he had worked on the train for a month at a time, working Winnipeg–Toronto–Halifax.

Back in our bedroom, we found bunks wider and longer than any on board our boats, for these coaches' size enables Charles's 6ft 4in to lie stretched out. Bed-head lights and shelves, little pouches for watches or rings, we had it all, and slept soundly on good track to the faint mooing at level crossings of the distant locomotive.

We woke to sunshine on the St Lawrence as the train took us up the river's southern side, past one French village after another, and little fenced farms or rural businesses, for this was the old settled part of French Quebec, where *habitants* have cultivated and subdivided the family land for generations. Delightfully, we got up at Trois Pistoles and breakfasted at St Philippe de Neri. By breakfast-time in the dining-car we realised that we were on a type of long-distance train that died out in Europe with the last war, the present-day equivalent of the Orient Express of glorious memory, or of the South African trains that used to take Charles as a boy on his 48-hour journey from Johannesburg to Cape Town for seaside holidays. Made up at Truro, Nova Scotia, from sections starting at Halifax and

North Sydney, the train runs to Montreal, whence a part continues via Winnipeg to Vancouver.

Four kinds of sleeping accommodation are offered: (a) bedrooms like ours; (b) single-berthed roomettes; (c) upper and lower curtained bunks running parallel to the central gangway (whence had come grunts and snores and children's squeals as we had passed through the night before on the way to our Mooseheads) which convert to seats by day; (d) cheaper still Dayniter coaches, with retractable seats and extending leg-rests, blankets and pillows being available from an attendant.

With a high standard of comfort, the train staffing was old-fashionedly lavish – and old-fashionedly polite. For railway buffs we give the make-up and staff as told us by our chief steward friend. The train has a diesel locomotive; sealed baggage car; baggage-dormitory car, which included 14 roomettes for train staff; four day coaches; a cafe-lounge car (ie a snack-bar or *casse-croute* car); two Dayniters; a dining-car/lounge-car, and three sleeping cars which include sections (parallel bunks), roomettes and bedrooms. And at the back of the train there is the delight of a look-out window where one can watch the country on both sides and the ever-receding track. There is a driver and fireman, conductor and two trainmen, baggage man, snack-bar steward and waiter, Dayniter attendant, dining-car steward, three waiters, chef, cook and cook-assistant, sleeping-car attendant and three porters.

This, we said to ourselves as we sat down to breakfast, is the way to travel, and tried to remember when last we had eaten bacon and eggs on a train. It must have been on the old steam-hauled Cheltenham Spa Express, running non-stop from Kemble (where we joined it) to Paddington.

Our bedroom bunks put away and armchairs restored, we settled back to watch Quebec Province go by, to read station names at the stops, make notes on fields and buildings, and seek land glimpses of the river and mountains we had seen from the water weeks ago. Fan moving the air, ventilation keeping down the heat, conscious of a bar in the next car, we couldn't care less when we got to Montreal. And all for one-third off normal fares, because we are senior citizens. Anxiously enquiring at Saint

John whether the concession applied to the English, we were told that age alone counted; carefully reaching for our passports to prove it, they were waved aside: 'what you've said is enough for me', the ticket clerk told us. Why do people with experience of life and time to spare sit around in airports, or motor down expressways, when they can spend it like this?

'Are we coming up to Quebec?' we asked the woman with four children who were all looking out of the corridor window.

'Oh, no,' she says, 'we don't get there till three o'clock.'

'Isn't it Montreal at three o'clock?' we say carefully.

'Aren't they the same thing?' she replies. She'd better not let Mr Lévesque hear her say that.

A good, nicely served dining-car lunch, over the Richlieu River on the bridge under which we had passed in *New Shoreham* on our way to Chambly, then past the Seaway's St Lambert lock, over the St Lawrence to see the city's towers beyond, and we were in Montreal on time. Good for VIA.

'Welcome to Montreal,' said the French-Canadian taxi-driver.

'We're glad to be back,' we replied. 'We've now visited three provinces of Canada, Quebec, Ontario and New Brunswick.'

'Canada must remain one,' he burst out. 'Canadians must live together, work together, seek the future together.'

His vehemence surprised us. We of course agreed with him, whereupon he pointed out every sight, gave us every street name, between the station and the hotel.

With him in mind, we chose a small French restaurant for our last night in the country. Should you wish to follow our example, seek out Le Paris Restaurant on St Catherine's Street. The pretty waitress spoke French with a dash of English; we spoke English with a dash of French, and over an excellent tournedos and a bottle of Macon we toasted Canada.

Next morning, from the Windsor station of the Canadian Pacific, blessed once more with blue skies, we caught the Amtrak train for New York. Here again at Montreal was railway magnificence, expressed architecturally in the days when railways were as supreme in their business as are airways now. A great five-tiered building with a tall tower, its exterior leaves a faintly cathedral-like impression, as though railways and church were parallel in permanence. Beside it towers the CP-owned Chateau Champlain Hotel, the Union Jack flying alongside the flags of Canada, Quebec and the United States. Today the Canadian Pacific company, still running a busy freight railway, has diversified far beyond its beginnings to become one of Canada's greatest conglomerates.

We climbed on board the *Adirondack*, Amtrak's 11.35am air-conditioned, turbo-liner train for New York. Out of Montreal over the spreading St Lawrence, here perhaps four times the width of the Thames in London, and then over the Seaway below Côte Ste Catherine lock, we ran through quiet country, first on Canadian Pacific tracks and then on those of the Napierville Junction Railway, to the border at Rouses Point, where we entered the United States for the fourth and last time on our journeyings, and moved to the rails of the Delaware & Hudson.

Past buttercupped meadows of hay and groups of black-and-white cows under trees, the ground began to gather itself in rolls as we came to Plattsburgh. Over a river, and the top of long, narrow Lake Champlain stretched away to our left, Vermont beyond; a lake 107 miles long, 1 to 13 miles broad, lying deep in the Adirondacks to the west and the Green Mountains to the east. Now began as lovely a train journey as one can take. For most of the way the track winds along the lake shore, out to the water, in through red-rocked cuttings, always by lakeside spruce, silver birch, alder, poplar, maple and elm, the foothills of the Adirondacks above. The lake is dotted with islands, and along the shore are cottages, marinas and piers, some with large moored barges, for the lake is accessible from the Hudson by way of the large Champlain branch of the New York State Barge Canal.

The line's windings increase as the lake edge grows steeper, and we watch the leading car turn left, then right, then left again, the whole a spectacular engineering feat of the 1870s when it was built. Near Wilsboro, Burlington in Vermont can be seen across the lake (a cross-lake ferry leaves from nearby Port Kent). Near Burlington, at the Shelburne open-air museum, the 220ft long sidewheel steamer *Ticonderoga*, which ceased operation in 1955, has found a home. At Willsboro we leave the lake for little English-looking farm fields among trees, and the small, brown, rocky Bouquet River, then return to it at Westport. Across the cloud-reflecting lake are the hills, and beyond them the Green Mountains, the Camel's Hump and Mount Mansfield prominent. So it goes on for two hours and more until, past Fort Ticonderoga (one can see the restored, star-shaped fort best after having passed the station) the lake narrows more and more and the country flattens. At Whitehall the Champlain branch waterway begins, one barge-lock right alongside the track.

The train now runs through easier country: we pass Saratoga Springs, a spa that combines health-giving with an interest in the performing arts and horse-racing, then seemingly through the main street of Mechanicville, junction for the Boston & Maine (freight yards filled with trucks carrying eastern names: Maine Central, Vermont Railway, Bangor & Aristook) until, suddenly crossing the Hudson, it stops at Albany-Rensselaer where we joined our fourth set of tracks, the Penn Central.

Thereafter another water route opens, as the track parallels the Hudson River on its eastern side. Now from the land we saw the Catskill Mountains once more; mansions, West Point, marinas, and always the grand lines of the hills of the western bank. Yachts were out, an occasional towboat pushed a barge, a crowded evening trip-boat passes. For over a hundred miles, as the declining sun gleamed on the still water, we ran beside the river until, as we turned left to follow the Harlem River's bank into New York, the last glowing rays lit up the high buildings ahead while we moved in half-darkness below. The train slowed for its terminus, and we ended a day that had in perfect weather combined our pleasure in waterways with our interest in railways. It had been a jewel of a day.

At 8.30pm the *Adirondack* stopped in Grand Central station. Skilful now in finding a redcap for our heavy suitcases, we trotted after him. Yellow taxi, glimpse of sunsets along parallel canyons, and we were at our hotel, hot, tired, and wanting only supper and bed. We were thankful to find that

'Late Supper' started at 9pm (dinner had been at the normal American early hour). Quickly booking a table in the supper-room, we tottered to our bedroom – and straight into yet another battle with American plumbing, this time because it was period plumbing. There was the bath, with the drain dead in its centre, an arrangement hard upon the tenderer parts. There was a lever moving in a half-circle. Up, as we sadly discovered while still dressed, turned on the shower. But what put in the plug, so to speak, or was it already in? We ran the water, and found it was out – but how, oh how, did one put it in? Hungry and hot, we had a bath with the water coming in just a little faster than it went out.

Supper was splendid, in a room all red wallpaper, red plush chairs and sofas, and chandeliers, with earnest service. Our hotel, the Algonquin, was recommended to us because it was old-fashioned and literary like ourselves. It certainly has character. This includes a hotel cat called Hamlet, a concierge (not a bell captain or head porter) in a brown bowler hat, a liftman who drives the lift (elevator) with a handle, and the welcome check-out time of 3pm. It also has a reputation as a meeting-place of literary notabilities, that dates from the 'Round Table' of between the wars, from Alexander Woolcott, Robert Benchley, George S. Kaufman and Dorothy Parker. Happily we looked round, sure that we were among the great: some, indeed, from eccentricity of dress, exuberance of manner or effervescence of speech, must, we were sure, be literary types in the full flow of self-expression. Others looked as if they were being entertained, above their usual standards, by publishers or literary agents. Between us we have written nearly forty books, but here, under the chandeliers, drinking our modest half-bottle of Chablis, we humbly reflected that we would have to write a lot more before being worthy of the Algonquin's supper-room. Even if we weren't worthy, however, we enjoyed it.

Back in our room, moderately levitated, we ran our fingers over the controls of the air-conditioner – a small model of the mighty Wurlitzer cinema organs of our youth. Success gave us confidence. We were then faced with our bedside reading lamps, which the bellhop had turned on when we arrived. Most electric switches press up and down (American the reverse of English) or in and out, but some twiddle. We searched up and down for switches, press-bars or knobs. Despairingly, on hands and knees, we searched under the beds. Light-years later, under the bedside telephone, we found two tiny knobs which earlier we had thought were bells. Apprehensively, in case they were bells, we pushed. No result. Then we twiddled. Eureka: the lights went out. Far more exhausted than before, we sank to sleep. Only in the morning did we discover that the waste control for the bath, of the lift-up-and-down variety, was right outside it in a separate vertical tube, of the kind which Alice Mary remembered from her boarding-school bathrooms long ago, so period was it.

To us, arrival at Grand Central station had been exploration's end. Our three days in New York were not for sightseeing, but for resting and recollecting, seeing friends, and a little getting the feel of the place.

The feel of New York on July days, temperature in the mid-eighties? What can one do but note impressions, and those only of half a dozen streets? The woman in the coffee-house who replied to our question whether it would be open that evening: 'Lady, we are open twenty-two hours a day for seven days a week – and if there was an eighth day we'd be open on that'. A different coffee-house where we had lunch, where the kindly, elderly, bustling waitress called us 'honey' and 'dear', and gave prompt service in gruelling conditions. If anyone is interested in discovering how high a human decibel count can rise, let him seek out the Central Coffee Shoppe on West 47th Street in the rush-hour; it's quite remarkable.

In the little Bryant Park next the public library, where a jazz band was playing, one of us got talking to an ex-Romanian who had fought under Patton in the last war, the other to a coloured man from Jamaica (not the island; a part of New York). The contrast of interesting old buildings in the side streets with modernity in the avenues, and the oddity that one hardly notices the skyscrapers except at the end of a vista, because their upper parts are above the level of usual vision. That the sky is something special looked at on street crossings or in squares. That 42nd Street and Broadway exhibit competitive and comprehensive sex: 'Eight sex acts at one time live on stage' (what, in this heat!). 'Girls, $10, no extras'. That there is no more hurry and bustle in New York than in London (except in the coffee-houses), but a lot more loitering, wandering, idling, by all races and in several languages: enough to make the visitor a trifle wary. Little shows or musicians on an occasional corner, flowers for sale everywhere, make walking pleasant. The multitude of taxis, and the inconspicuousness of subway stations. The cheerful sight of the Stars and Stripes up and down the streets. As elsewhere in the States, the absence of public lavatories (people use these in department stores, restaurants, museums or whatnot) and of identifiable sub-post offices. The street noise coming from the main avenues, even to the twelfth floor in a side street, a noise punctuated on our visit by tremendous bangs, for, as in London at Guy Fawkes time, fireworks are let off before the Fourth of July arrives. Punctuated also by the extraordinary menagerie noises given off by the New York police-cars, ambulances and fire-engines. And the query why locals call the city The Big Apple. And the curious ambiguity of the city's place in the national consciousness, so that we could see a lecture announced as 'Does the United States need New York?' and that those who do not live there say nothing would induce them to do so, and its inhabitants swear nothing would make them leave.

One sight we did not miss, however. When, long ago, Alice Mary had been a graduate student at Mount Holyoke College, Massachusetts, she had spent a vacation working in Doubleday Doran's bookshop in Grand Central Station. So back to it we went. Here, incarnate, is our forefathers' philosophical idea of a railway station. Surely, among the many mansions of heaven, a celestial Grand Central will be thronged with all those who have worked on, travelled on, loved railways. It is incomparable. The high balustraded frontage rises from 42nd Street at Vanderbilt Avenue, surmounted by statuary centred on a standing figure of Mercury, god of travel, borne on the wings of an eagle.

One passes through a high portico lit by bulb chandeliers into the main concourse, so high that it seems the sky indeed is the limit, for the distant grey-blue ceiling is a representation of the sky, its stars and constellations. From one end a grand double staircase sweeps up to street level; at one side an enormous clock, tuned to Big Ben, strikes the quarters with sounds that penetrate the whole building. Because it was the Saturday morning of the Fourth of July weekend, there were queues at the booking offices buying holiday tickets, and a longer one for the Amtrak Empire State Express to Buffalo. Along subways leading to surrounding streets are the track entrances, in themselves impressive, but by themselves dwarfed.

Yet the great concourse is only the middle of three levels: below is another smaller one, with more track entrances; above, an interior balcony that becomes an external balustrade.

In the concourses, and along the subways with their ornate metal hanging lamps, are the lights of a small circular town of shops. Doubleday Doran's bookshop was no more, but there were others. Shops also of many kinds, restaurants, a bank if you needed money, a stockbroker's office for immediate advice upon that snip you had noticed while reading the *Wall Street Journal* in the train, and places to buy tickets for all sports and entertainments, to risk dollars in a lottery, or have a flutter on the horses at OTB (off track betting). Paraphrasing Dr Johnson, we felt that a man who has seen Grand Central – even now, when railways have fallen from their high estate – has seen New York. Satisfied, we went to lunch.

On our last evening we walked for a stretch round Lexington and Madison Avenues, amidst the trash and litter of Saturday, thinking of our travels and the pleasures and strangenesses we had found. Back in the hotel a waiter we knew was sitting in his white coat in the lounge by the door, off duty but watching the crowd. We spoke to him, found he was a Cypriot, once an interpreter in Greek and English, was often in England, his mother living in Hornsey, London. We had again that clear American sense of talking person to person.

No shape had imposed itself upon our impressions of New

York when our taxi came next morning to take us to the QE2 at the passenger-ship terminal. Two hours later we were doing what very many before us have done, but few after will do, watching from the deck of an Atlantic liner the skyscrapers, the Statue of Liberty, and the Verrazano Bridge fade slowly astern. We watched until nothing was left to be seen. Then we went below.

What fun we had had.

The Statue of Liberty fades astern . . .

Further Information

Cruise addresses:

Delta Queen Steamboat Company
511 Main Street
Cincinnati
Ohio 45202
USA

American Canadian Line Inc
PO Box 368
Warren
RI 02885
USA

(Note: *New Shoreham*, on which we travelled, has been replaced by *New Shoreham II*)

A list of boat trips in the United States can be sought from Dr W. E. Trout, American Canal Society, 1932 Cinco Robles Drive, Cal 91010, USA. Please send him an international reply coupon.

Publications on American canals are available from the American Canal and Transportation Center, Box 310, Shepherdstown, WV 25443.

The American Canal Society has many British members. Secretary, Charles W. Derr, 117 Main Street, Freemansburg, PA 18017.

A general book on American canal history is H. S. Drago's *Canal Days in America* (1972) and on that of Canada, Robert F. Legget's *Canals of Canada* (1976). The latter is available from David & Charles.